A Boy's-Eye View
of World War II
and Other Reminiscences
of Maryland's
Eastern Shore

Frank H. Pierce

HERITAGE BOOKS
2007

HERITAGE BOOKS

AN IMPRINT OF HERITAGE BOOKS, INC.

Books, CDs, and more—Worldwide

For our listing of thousands of titles see our website
at
www.HeritageBooks.com

Published 2007 by
HERITAGE BOOKS, INC.
Publishing Division
65 East Main Street
Westminster, Maryland 21157-5026

Other books by the author:
The Tagebuch of Ernst Silge, USN

International Standard Book Number: 978-0-7884-0886-0

Dedication

This book, along with many of the memories contained within it, is dedicated to my maternal grandmother, Anna Matilda Brown (1884-1959). a woman of no pretense and modest ambitions, but one who believed that one's interests in intellectual pursuits should never find themselves intimidated by a lack of academic degrees. She served as Mayor of Princess Anne from 1940 to 1948 and was, so far as research can reveal, the first woman to be elected in her own right as the head of government in an incorporated town in the United States.

Preface
A Boy's Eye View Of World War II
And Other Reminiscences
of Maryland's Eastern Shore

Save for those who grew up in the general area of the Chesapeake Bay, the name Princess Anne, Maryland will mean little. Be it sufficient to say at this time that it is a small town, set almost equally in good farming land and salt water marsh, located fairly down the Delmarva Peninsula, the area which forms home to nine Maryland counties, two more from Virginia, and the entire state of Delaware.

It was, and remains today, a very small town, with slightly more than one-thousand people living within its corporate boundaries. It defies generalization. At the same time, it is much poorer than many towns and suburban areas of similar size. It is also much more well-to-do and prosperous. It all depends on your point of view.

During World War II, save for its geography, Princess Anne could have been located in any part of the United States. It could have been on the outskirts of Richmond, Indiana, or a small town north of Milwaukee, or an agricultural village north of San Francisco or Cape May, New Jersey. The names of the people and the merchants' stores are different, of course. But all the reader need do is bring back from memory or dredge up from imagination his own set of names. They're all there, all in place, even to the boy who, fifty years later, wrote it all down before the memories fade. It's not a story of geography but of attitudes. And in that crisis time, attitudes were universal.

Most of the following stories in one form or another, were published at various times in the Somerset Herald *in Princess Anne through the cooperation of Mr. Richard Crumbacker, Editor. The first story, A Boy's Eye View of World War II, copyright 1988, was published in slightly modified form by Atlantic Publishing Company and was made available in a soft paperback edition by the Somerset County Historical Trust. The Trust has given permission for the use of this material with its present expansion.*

Frank H. Pierce, III
Silver Spring, MD
29 July, 1997

The Twenty-Ninth Division Stands Ready to
Defend the Presbyterian Sunday School
Against Nazi Invasion
January 15 1942

A Boy's-eye View of World War II

Princess Anne during the War Years

As we grow older, we become more forgetful. It's not just the process of aging which makes us miss by five the year in which we took the vacation in Maine or to completely forget the name of the people who lived next door back when we bought the house. By fifty or sixty, we've got so many memories stored away that the names and dates get all scrambled in our minds. Not so when we are very young. The mind is like a steel trap. Nothing, once captured, ever escapes. For sheer total recall of all kinds of facts, trivial and worthwhile, it's hard to beat the mind of a ten-year old. Psychologists tell us this is true, but we don't need them. We've all been there once ourselves.

I was lucky, therefore, to have been born in 1931 because when I was ten years old it was 1941. That was the year the big War began for all of us in Princess Anne. I know that the War was already more than two years old but that was in Europe and it was far away. Unless you'd found yourself ram-rodded into uniform in the one-year military draft which actually got started in 1940, the War didn't make much of an impression. Things went on in Princess Anne pretty much like they'd always gone on forever, I guessed.

Actually,the war in Europe did make changes but they were ever so slight and they got lost in the course or our day-to-day living at Princess Anne Elementary School. Still, I can remember back when it all started, not Pearl Harbor, but the real war, the one in Europe. It was Labor Day weekend of 1939, of course, a time for people in Princess Anne to take one last run to Ocean City, splash in the Atlantic, and eat too much salt-water taffy. We did, my grandmother, me, and our next door neighbor, Miss Julia Hanley. I worked hard that day to be better behaved than I generally was. Miss Hanley was slated to be my third-grade teacher, come Tuesday morning and the opening of school.

We got back about dusk and my grandmother was in the old back kitchen of her house, fixing dinner when we both heard someone rapping on the window overlooking the little spring house. By now it was black outside, but I saw Miss Hanley's face, agitated, holding up a copy of the Baltimore Evening Sun. She was pointing to the banner headlines and from the light from the window I could make out the words: HITLER INVADES POLAND. "We're all going to be in it now," she said.

I could read the words well enough. Somewhere I'd seen the word "Hitler" and I sounded out "Invades" and sort of gave up on the last word, but the meaning wasn't lost on me. This was big, important stuff, and I told myself that I wasn't going to be left out. I'd better learn to read in a hurry.

Right away I began to read the papers, the Hearst Papers *Baltimore American* being my favorite because it had more pictures and more exciting headlines than the more reputable *Sunpapers*. And every Sunday there was the great, sensational Sunday Supplement, all devoted to the War with a garish caricatured war map on the front of each edition. By mid-September, I had pinned the first one to the bedroom wall. "Will Nazi Bombers Blast Britain's Hope?" I liked it because it showed big, fearsome German airplanes flying across the map of France straight for England. It was that sort of thing that I, at eight years old, related to very easily. I learned much of my European geography early, watching first one and then another country disappear from the Hearst war maps.

The *Weekly Reader,* our Window-on-the-World in Miss Hanley's Third Grade, told us of the German invasion of Holland. I learned a little heart-rending popluar song about two little war refugees girls called *My Sister and I.* But for most of us, the war was far away and paled by comparison with the heady excitement of being crammed into the still-unfinished Washington High School building after the elementary school had burned down in the summer of 1939.

And sometime around that period, our particular way of saluting the American Flag during the opening-exercise Pledge of Allegiance came into official disfavor. During the first and second grades we stood at the best imitation of Attention we could muster, hands over hearts, and said "I pledge allegiance ..." Well and good, but on the next words "... to the Flag ...", we snapped out our tiny arms toward the banner, straight armed, palms up, a small group of sunny-faced American kids from Princess Anne giving a fair-to-good imitation of a Nazi salute to Old Glory.

This was repeated, day after day, throughout the length and breadth of America, and it was nothing more than the way most American children had always saluted the flag forever, so far as most people knew. But considering the disrepute into which Fascism was falling, the effect, pictorially, was unnerving to say the least. The dictum came down: No more stiff-arm salutes. Get those little hands over your hearts and keep them there, all the way through Liberty and Justice for All!

But our world-view wasn't very cosmopolitan. It centered mostly on the town and family and Saturday movies and recess and marble games and only such geography and history as we were absolutely compelled to master. I don't believe there was a single one of us in Miss Lois Jackson's fifth-grade class at Princess Anne Elementary School who could have located Pearl Harbor on the map before our Pacific Fleet was bombed on the seventh of December of that year. We were too busy memorizing the names of each of the county seats in Maryland to concern ourselves overly much with such foreign stuff. But on the eighth, everybody knew.

As her contribution to the war which she and everyone else felt was fast coming, Miss Jackson had been scheduling a little current-events session in opening exercises each morning. A few of us could remember some scrap of what we'd heard on the radio news each morning and we'd parrot back to her our imperfect recollections of the event ... last night's bombing of London or the dreaded German drive toward Moscow.

But the eighth of December was different. Hands waved. No one was shy. "What happened yesterday?" she asked in the most matter-of-fact voice I could imagine. Milbourne Witt got the nod.

"The Japs bombed Pearl Harbor!" he sputtered, sure for once that he was on solid ground.

"Yes," she said. And that was that.

* * *

I don't know when and where he had heard the news but I remember clearly where I was. It began in Henry Morris's restaurant up on Main Street. It was a clear, mild December afternoon. I'd spent the morning at home filling out my final Christmas list from the special Sears and Roebuck Christmas wish book. Around one in the afternoon I found a spare nickel and decided to spend it on a Coke before Sunday grew any older. The juke box was playing a current hill-billy favorite. The song was, as it turned out, suddenly pathetically dated even as the coin hit the slot. "*I'll be back in a year, little darlin'*," the words went, "*Uncle Sam has called my name*".

I looked out across the street, across to the Esso station. I was mildly puzzled. There, in knots of three or four were soldiers, these one-year draftees, hitch-hiking south, back to Camp Somerset at Westover. This was a seven-PM phenomenon, not a one-thirty-in the-afternoon happening. Thus it had always been since they converted Somerset from a CCC Camp to an Army camp a year before. Sundays meant a pass and these fellows always stayed in town until the last minute. That much I knew. But it was still early afternoon. I considered that I was too young to really understand soldiers.

It wasn't until later, about three o'clock, when I walked up on my Grandmother's porch that she told me what had happened. Mother and Dad were still outside in the car and I'd run inside to tell her that we were waiting for her. "They've bombed Pearl Harbor," she said. "We're at war now. Not just Europe. All of us." She'd been listening to the little table radio in the dining room when the news had come through.

Then she and I walked outside together and I blurted out the news to Dad and Mother as I climbed into the back seat. None of us seemed particularly distressed or excited. Even to me it wasn't a surprise. It wasn't a sudden unexpected thrusting of our country into war. Rather it was only the ultimate step in a series of escalations into the war we all felt would come. I'd followed the news of the sinking of the United States destroyer *Reuben James* by Nazi U boats and I knew about the Lend-Lease Program where we had promised to let Great Britain have some of our overaged destroyers left over from the First World War. So far as any ten-year old boy in Princess Anne was concerned, Hitler was already the enemy and we knew it and were as certain of the truth of it as we were certain of our Bible stories from Sunday School. That we were not at war was, I guessed, a technicality that would all work itself out. The war news for the past sixteen months news had made all of us philosophical and resigned.

And then we took one of our typical Sunday afternoon drives up by Allen and Loretta Station, just as we always did, in Dad's new `41 Chevy coupe. It was a clear and mild afternoon down on the Chesapeake that day, and I recall looking out of the right window and thinking that the landscape looked just the same, war or no war. Gas was still as available as Gunther's Beer at Henry's. It had not yet been declared unpatriotic to pleasure-drive.

* * *

The war changed Princess Anne and the changes weren't long in coming. People in Washington soon realized that this war wouldn't be like other wars. Aircraft could and had crossed the Atlantic without refueling. Submarine warfare had risen to heights of technical perfection unimagined in the First World War. It was possible if not probable that war might actually come to the shores of America. And located as we were on the East Coast, it would most likely come to us first.

The Shore needed some line of defense, and what better use could be made of the thousands of inductee- soldiers just finishing basic training than to post them strategically in various towns and villages? Princess Anne was selected for its own company of field artillery and within weeks of Pearl Harbor, a unit of the Twenty-ninth Blue-and-Gray Division arrived.

I was never sure precisely how the Army would have deployed these young fellows if they were ever needed to defend these shores. The company itself was an old-line National Guard unit from Richmond, Virginia with a history that pre-dated the Civil War. It was commanded by a trim, blond all-together military-looking first lieutenant from the regular army named Martin. The troops were youngish Southern boys, mostly in their late teens and new at the soldiering occupation. Hardly a one of them had risen to the rank of Private First Class. Their field artillery consisted, as I recall, of a single 37-mm field piece.

Princess Anne wasn't basically set up for soldiering. We used the only open piece of land in town for their bivouac ... the land over across Beechwood Street where, until 1938, the old Washington High School had stood. It was then nothing more than what it remained for years, a hard-packed open field. Our recruits rapidly got used to the idea of living and sleeping in Army tents.

There was no place over on the "old school grounds", as it was called, to cook and eat so the elders of the Manokin Presbyterian Church made the Church Lecture Room available to them as a mess hall. The "Lecture Room" was the official name, but to most of us it was the Sunday School room. It sat, looking about the same then as today, on the north-west corner of Beechwood and Prince William Street.

There wasn't much to keep these three or four score of young boys busy and out of trouble. The Germans hadn't invaded. So Lieutenant Martin kept them occupied with all sorts of imaginative drilling and other soldierly things. He posted guards at the Sunday School, the water tower, Court House and other strategic points in town, sometimes doubling them up, sometimes keeping a twenty-four hour posting. They issued frighteningly proper military challenges to local people whose business required them to pass. He marched and counter--marched the relief guards up and down Beechwood Street. Martin's theory was that a soldier on guard duty would stay out of trouble.

These young soldiers were a source of great fascination. For one thing, they all carried rifles. A rifle bigger than a twenty-two was something of supreme interest to me. I wasn't the least disappointed that these were World War One 1903A1 Springfields, the old bolt-action, five-shooter kinds and not the new, semi- automatic Garand M-1. My expectations weren't too high in those days. They carried clips of 30-06 caliber rimless cartridges in their web belts strapped over their heavy olive-drab overcoats. They looked like they meant business. I'd stop and stare every time I passed the Sunday School room.

Every evening at sundown, the entire company, minus guards, which were considerable in number, trooped up to the Court House lawn. There they made a great ceremony of lowering the Flag according to military protocol. The two platoons drew up Prince William Street in a wondrous military clatter, rifles at right- shoulder arms, with lots of column-right orders from the sergeants.

It was the high point of my day. It seems that I was always on hand, along with Jack Keller, Francis Panzer, Dick Layfield, and perhaps Preston Tyler to watch this magnificent spectacle. We'd generally stand on the Main Street side, mackinaw jacket collars high, shivering in the fading light of late winter. The First Sergeant, whose name as I recall was "Pee-Wee", would bark the orders. It was his show. Then a barely adequate bugler came front and center and played "Retreat", the traditional bugle call for the lowering of colors. Last came the ceremonial folding of the Flag into the traditional tricorn, another flurry of shouted commands, Order-Arms, Right shoulder-Arms, Left-face, Forward-March! It was grand.

Later at nine o'clock, from my house at Beechwood and Washington Avenue, I'd hear the bugle from across the tracks play Tatoo, then Taps. Lieutenant Martin got his charges into bed early, no question. Princess Anne welcomed the boys with open arms and the sort of hospitality which you would have expected in those days. Sundays meant Sunday dinner with one or two of the soldiers. The Episcopalians made the Parish House available as a sort of a make-shift USO as I remember. Girls who were far too old for me to know well put on bright red lipstick and little pill-box hats and dated soldiers. Girls around my age who should have known better and who would have been skinned by their parents if they'd talked about dating still got in on the excitement by swearing to one and all that they were deeply in love with at least one soldier. I believed them implicitly. But it always gave me a sinking feeling. How could I compete, at ten, with a soldier from the United States Army?

The Twenty-ninth was organized around the National Guard of the states of Virginia and Maryland and these were almost like Princess Anne boys, watermen and farmers and small-town fellows who fitted in as though they'd been born and raised in Somerset County. But in the spring, after their fair share of marching and counter-marching up and down Antioch Avenue they were replaced by another artillery company from Pennsylvania's Twenty-eighth, the Keystone division.

These men were under the command of a wiry little no-nonsense Captain named Hildebrand who came from Harrisburg. He wore starched shirts, had a bristling black mustache and always sported a pair of fancy wire-rimmed aviator sunglasses, the kind which hardly anybody in Princess Anne ever wore unless he went to Ocean City. The soldiers were from far-away exotic places like Pittsburgh and Scranton and Altoona and had names like Kolakowski, Piacezzi, and Rosenkranz. Almost immediately I missed the Twenty-ninth Division.

During off hours, they soon occupied Henry Morris's restaurant and Carey's soda fountain and the soda fountain at Dougherty and Hayman's drug store. Roy Alder, who owned and maintained all of the juke boxes for miles around, soon found appropriate music for Henry's Wurlitzer, and before I knew it, Polish polkas had occupied at least twelve of the twenty-four slots. I never hear the song *Rosamunda* today that I am not reminded of the summer of 1942, a pink-faced Pennsylvanian dropping another nickel in the slot and teaching one of our local girls more than she ever really wanted to know about how to polka.

But they were good fellows, these Pennsylvanians, just different from the Virginians. It took us a little longer to get used to them. Back then, the world was more or less judged by how we on the Shore viewed the world.

The Pennsylvanians opened their Sunday-school mess hall one rainy Saturday afternoon to all of the youngsters in town. They put on songs and skits for us and we loved it. They gave each of a dozen or so of us boys a piece of C-Ration hardtack and told us to eat it as fast as possible, the winner being he who could first whistle the Caissons-go-Rolling-Along. Somehow I managed to win, surprising myself totally because I never knew how to whistle before. A sergeant gave me my prize, a glass Liberty Bell savings bank.

One must understand the impression which this and other things about these soldiers made on us. This was real, not comic book stuff. They wore all kinds of great uniforms, starched khakis in the summer, magnificent military jackets in the winter. And stripes and hash marks and Corps insignia and scarlet artillery piping on their caps. And the officers, the few that we saw, were even more magnificent. They wore Sam Browne belts, and had many more buttons which were much more intricately wrought. They had a dress uniform called "Pinks" which wasn't pink at all but sort of dusty rose and brown. On duty, officers carried .45-caliber automatic pistols which we told each other were the most deadly gun in the world, the kind that would blow a Jap in two if you caught him at the right spot in his middle.

Sometime in the early spring of `forty-two the fifth and sixth grade boys decided that uniforms were much better than knickers and wooly sweaters so we began to collect odds and ends and cast-offs. When the corporal made his promotion to sergeant, his first act was to rip off a perfectly good pair of corporal's stripes and throw his old double-stripes away just like they were so much junk.

That was foolish, we felt. Those old strips were just the thing to spiffy up a windbreaker, particularly if you could find a Keystone division red shoulder patch to wear above it. An Overseas cap was obligatory. And if a pair of corporal's stripes made your jacket more elegant, why not add a few more, just for good measure? Private's stripes on top of corporals made you look just like a sergeant. Heavy layers of used overseas stripes and hash marks and wound stripes filled in any un-chevroned gap. Then you'd top the whole thing off with a too-big overseas cap. And if these weren't enough, you could resort to buying things. The Mart Men's Store next door to Holland's barbershop sold insignia and uniform equipments and they always kept a fascinating window display of all things imaginable which could dress up the jacket of any one of us.

We were Army by loyalty in Princess Anne in 1942. We had our own private army. Army Loyalty backed by Army Insignia was the motto of our sixth grade. Jack Keller and I vied for military supremacy but I was never in the same league with him and I finally gave up trying.

Posters such as these steeled the Home Front of Princess Anne for a long and arduous war. They were also representative of how the boys in the sixth grade of Princess Anne Elementary School envisioned themselves.

Jack had developed his own private pipeline to military grandeur. During the entire year of 1942 he had the wonderful fortune to find himself in love with Patsy Ward.

Patsy had the curliest hair and best freckles of any girl in our class. This alone could have sufficed for Jack but she had one other supreme distinction which set her apart from all other girls. Her father was Melvin Ward. Melvin Ward was the owner of Melvin Ward's Texaco station and grill right across Route 13 from Camp Somerset. Ward's was the closest store to the main gate and was the soldiers' prime source of non- military coffee and hamburgers.

Where others might have to search and barter for used insignia, Patsy Ward came naturally by these treasures and they washed over her in a flood, not just common run-of-the mill infantry and artillery insignia but the rare and exotic, the Finance Corps, Intelligence, and goodness-knows what other sorts of esoterica. Patsy gave Jack the lion's share of this trove. Jack owned a blue mackinaw which attested to the fact that he belonged to at least three separate army divisions, was a top sergeant-corporal in the infantry- tank corps, had been wounded seven times in France and had a total service time of thirty-three years, not a bad record for a ten year-old.

Later, it became more and more permissible to demonstrate fidelity to the Navy, particularly after the Naval Air Station at Chincoteague was activated and a white hat properly rolled, salted, and squared was a thing you could be proud of. But during those first months, our loyalties to the Army were as strong as General Pershing's.

* * *

My favorite reading was a used paper-backed book given to me by a soldier in the 29th. It was titled, directly enough, The *New Soldier's Handbook*. Inside were more than a hundred pages of all the colorful things which a new soldier was supposed to know. Within weeks I knew them all. I could dig a latrine. I understood the accepted use of a stretcher and how to tell the sergeant from the Lieutenant. I knew how to use two machine guns to establish a converging field of fire in case I had to defend my position against the Germans. I read of and was properly impressed by the ravages of VD and knew how to hang a Lister bag for drinking water. I was pretty sure I would have known how to field-strip a Springfield rifle but nobody would let me have one to find out.

But deep inside, when the troops weren't mustering on the Court House lawn or crunching and rattling their way up Beechwood Street and the Army seemed momentarily far away, the Spring of 1942 was a frightening time for all of us. Any of us old enough to read the papers knew everything that our elders knew. And on the whole, what we read and what we heard wasn't reassuring at all.

The *Baltimore Morning Sun* was delivered each morning to our front porch and I early on developed the habit of reading the front pages as well as the funnies. The humiliation of Bataan Peninsula was still weighing heavily on me one morning when I read, front page, that a German invasion of the east coast, if it came at all, wouldn't come before mid-summer when the Atlantic was calm. If that three-month reprieve was intended to reassure me, it failed miserably. Today this reads like blatant hysteria. Then it was simply the news in the Sunpapers.

Elton Ross's barber shop was the open forum for all sorts of war news and commentary. Always of a Saturday, I'd see three or four of the town elders ... Mr. Mace Smith, Sam Sudler, Walter Long ... sitting and waiting for a chair. These were men of consequence, I knew, and what they said carried a lot of weight with me. They'd brood silently over the barber shop copy of the Sun. The war maps were always centered above the fold just under the headlines, showing the positions of the front lines of two or three theaters of war. The Axis was in black and we were in white. Every day there seemed to be less and less white. They'd look at it for a while, shaking their heads. "What do you think about the war?" they'd ask each other. "I don't know. I just don't know," they'd always answer. I knew that they knew. They just didn't want to say.

I was cheered considerably by the Battle of Midway in May and then again by our invasion of Guadalcanal in August but I was the optimist in our group. To me, Midway was a turning point. But too much optimism was equated with a lack or resolve, or lack of "stick-
-to-it-iveness". "Things'll get worse before they get better," one of my teachers cautioned me sternly. As it turned out, however, I was more right than she. And besides, summer had come and gone and the Germans hadn't invaded, *Baltimore Sun* notwithstanding.

As in all wars up to that time, the newspapers were used not so much to inform us at any great level of military understanding as to condition us and keep up morale on what was then called "the Home Front". That the news would be censored and managed was assumed and accepted by all. We would have considered an editor to be a traitor if he printed every secret he was privy to.

We laughed at the dozens of cartoons portraying our Axis enemies as three little caricatures standing cheek to jowl like the Three Stooges... Hitler, Mussolini, and The Jap, they were usually labeled. Early on, Japan had no one of sufficient pre-eminence to identify by name so they took no chances and made him a generic Jap.

Among my friends, the Germans were feared and dreaded. They seemed to be supermen who ran relentlessly over opposing field armies and were always rumored to be on the verge of releasing some horrible secret weapon which their evil genius allowed them to develop. The Italians were there for laughs. People didn't take Mussolini seriously and they proved themselves right.

The villains in our comic books always had, naturally enough, a German accent. Germans we hated with a noisy, spontaneous and bombastic passion. We killed them by the thousands in mock-battles on Lankford's Hill. But we fell silent when somebody mentioned the Japs. The Japs we loathed.

For Freedom's Sake

BUY WAR BONDS

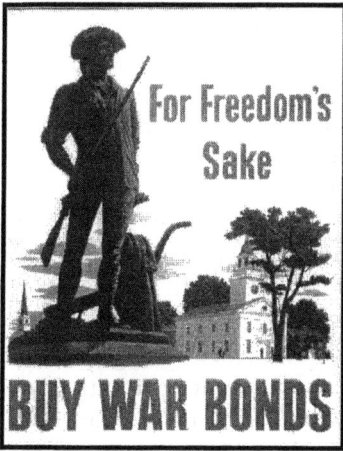

The Minute Man - Patriotism in increments of twenty-five cents

Nobody, not the newspapers nor radio, and least of all ourselves, called them Japanese. They were Japs. "Jap" was a word which you could use in public. Other names for our Eastern enemy were considerably less formal but more descriptive. In the Spring of 1942 we read the first of the atrocity stories in the papers, the Jap butchery and torture and Death March of our prisoners of war at Bataan Peninsula in the Philippines. We were told that Japs cared nothing for their own lives and certainly not for the lives of American prisoners. They were fanatics. War we could accept, but not fanaticism. Rules of War observed even by the evil Nazis were flagrantly broken by the Japs. It could all have been propaganda, issued by the Office of War Information to stiffen our resolve and make us buy War Bonds. But it wasn't. It was true. All of it.

But we bought war bonds and stamps anyway. Tuesday was stamp day and during opening exercises, one of the more capable seventh-grade girls would move class-to-class to collect our stamp money.

A stamp cost twenty-five cents, a sizable sum of money in those pre-inflation times. Each stamp bore the picture of the famous Minute Man statue. You collected stamps in your stamp book until you had $18.75 and then you could turn the book in for a war bond. In ten years the bond would be worth $25.00. This proposition was used time and time again to explain the standard sixth-grade arithmetic lessons on principal, rate, and interest.

Whether War Bonds directly helped the war effort as much as Washington said was questionable. But it did take money out of circulation and that in itself was good for the country. People were making money for the first time since the Great Depression. With money in hand, Americans wanted the things they'd not had for years. But the civilian goods just weren't available. Too much cash in our pockets, Washington knew, would send prices skyrocketing and ruin us in rampant inflation and a Black Market.

Prices were held in check through the efforts of one Leon Henderson, the greatest of all Washington Bureaucrats. He headed up the Office of Price Administration or OPA as it was called. The OPA had its fingers everywhere, they set wages and established ceiling prices for everything. They regulated and controlled. They were constantly in the papers. Leon Henderson single-handedly, as much as anybody, managed the American economy and we in Princess Anne, being an independent lot, hated the man's name and despised his agency. I overheard an angry mother threaten her misbehaving three-year old daughter in the American Store: "You better behave yourself, young lady, or the OPA's going to get you." What the OPA had to offer was a bitter but absolutely necessary dose of state-controlled medicine and we weren't about to take it without squirming.

But one happy benefit which came directly from the war was a decision by the Somerset County Board of Education to provide a summer vacation from May 15th to September 15th. Because so many of our young men had already enlisted in the services, farm labor was in short supply. If a farmer could get through spring planting by himself, the Board of Education could make high-schoolers available during the growing season and harvest.

The long summer vacation was not without cost. Saturday mornings found us at our desks with no recess. They broke us out at noon, hoping that we'd gotten a full day's worth of knowledge crammed into us. But it was of no avail. We wiggled and squirmed our way through the morning. After all, it was Saturday.

But if you lived in town as I did, you didn't have much, as sixth-graders, to contribute directly to the war effort anyway. So we worked hard on the morale end of things. I collected pictures of airplanes. Each month, *Air Trails*, my favorite among all magazines, printed a glorious full-color centerfold of a Spitfire or B-25 *Mitchell* or Grumman Wildcat. I pulled each one in turn and thumb-tacked it to the wall in front of my bed.

Jack Keller took a different approach. His wall was covered too, but mostly with drawings, intricate depictions of battles drawn on three-ring lined notebook paper. Portrayed were dogged air battles with Messerschmitts and Heinkels going down in flame under the guns of American planes. He generally drew more German planes than American planes because crosses were easier to draw than stars. He also drew pictures of fearsome sea battles with battleships and smoke. He was better at Navy things than I. I was the aircraft expert.

I wasn't alone. Almost all of the boys, and a few of the girls, built model airplanes. Hayman's drug store was the center for modelers. In a back corridor, Pete Hayman had devoted a few square feet to model airplanes and supplies, glue, dope, paper, and the like. For ten cents, I could buy a balsa-wood solid model made by Comet or a built-up flying model with rubber band motor. Either type promised a good three days of work. My first attempts produced lumpy-looking solid models and those which were supposed to fly didn't. But practice and a grand-mother who insisted that I meticulously follow the plans soon brought better results. Those which were good could be displayed. Periodically, Hayman's devoted the corner window on main street to the better models. At times, the handiwork of a good dozen local modelers were on proud display.

Christmas of 1942 was a frustrating time for those of us who remembered the wonderful toys and bicycles and cameras which were

available in 1941. The war theme was everywhere. Griffith's five-
-and-ten sold dolls which had been hurriedly re-costumed as war nurses
with blue capes and little red crosses. War- critical materials had been
removed from almost everything and what was left was shoddy and
second class. This was the year of the cardboard Christmas ornament.
The beautiful soft balsa which was featured in my Comet models all
summer was being gradually replaced by a grade of yellow pine which
would have challenged the blade of a bench saw. This material gave a
whole new definition to the term "softwood". DuPont acetate-cement
glue was replaced by a casein product from Bordon's which you had to
mix with water. It had the stick-ability of flour.

Somewhere along around this time, the Army decided that they need
aircraft recognition models and they provided solid models packaged
and sold by Storm-Becker, under the flawed assumption that the
creative energies of millions of ten-year olds across the United States
could be harnessed to produce accurate scale models suitable for
aircraft recognition training. The parts had been sawed into a general
likeness of the airplane in question but the wood had a hardness factor
somewhere between good grade carbon steel and tungsten. They gave
us directions to show us how to use a single-edge razor blade to cut and
shape the wood and templates to tell us when we'd worked it too much.
They gave us an address to which we could mail the finished model in
the unlikely event that we completed it.

The program was a total failure. Many of us tried. None of us, to my
knowledge, were successful. George Austin, who'd been building models
since before I could read, gave up on his and at that point I threw in
the towel. The Army Air Corps aircraft recognition program had to
soldier on manfully without the support of any of us.

* * *

But on occasion I'd meet up with a genuine airplane and this was an
unparalleled thrill. Once in early April of 1942, the savings bond
people offered to send the wreckage of a real German Messerschmitt Bf
109 fighter plane to town so that we could see just how effective it was
to buy war bonds and stamps and how good our airmen could be if

we'd just buy them bullets. They laid it out on a flatbed trailer. It was on tour, north to south, and was in Salisbury when I heard of it.

I resolved to sneak away from school the next day and steal a look at this trophy of war when it came through town. I had even smuggled my Agfa 616 camera to school that morning. I had a plan all ready and had convinced others in my class that we could make a fast, hidden run up to the Court House at noon, see the Messerschmitt and all be back in the school yard before the one o'clock bell rang. It was a good plan and we could have done it, probably, but unfortunately, Miss Jackson destroyed it. She dismissed the entire class and we all hiked, totally sanctioned, to the Court House.

We were a bit let down when, in place of the fearsome Messerschmitt, we saw, in front of the Court House, a flat-bed truck carrying a plain old run-of-the-mill U.S. Navy Wildcat fighter. Its condition told me it would never fly again. I was particularly disappointed because I was the one who had been touting the Messerschmitt display. Somehow I felt that this was all my fault. So did the others.

The Wildcat, until a few hours earlier, had been waist-deep in the mud of a dairy farm pasture up at Fruitland. It had plowed itself in the night before when a young Ensign misread his fuel tank selector switch. Norfolk Naval Air Station had hurriedly dispatched a truck to bring the wreckage home for possible repair and it was this truck which Police Chief Jim Revelle spotted coming down Route 13 from Salisbury.

Of all of his virtues, aircraft recognition never ranked high with Chief Revelle and so, in full uniform he flagged over the lone sailor at the wheel. "Hold her right here," he told the now worried young fellow. "We heard you were coming and I got orders to park you over yonder," he said, pointing to the roped off area in front of the Court House.

The young sailor protested a little bit but when Chief Revelle told him firmly that he was to park that truck "raht-thar" the youngster figured that the whole matter was bigger than he was and it was now an issue between the Town of Princess Anne and the U. S. Navy. He allowed as how he hadn't had any breakfast anyway and this looked like a good place to stop as any. Thus we came upon the scene: Grumman Wildcat in front of the Courthouse heading south, sailor in Carey's having a late breakfast, and Chief Revelle standing proudly beside the trailer, waiting to display his supposed Messerschmitt to all comers.

I couldn't figure it out but then someone looked up and coming down past Broad Street was another truck, this one flying a full rig of United States War Bond flags and regalia. And there, strapped to the bed, was the genuine shot-down Messerschmitt. It turned out right. Chief Revelle directed the second truck around the corner of Prince William Street and I climbed all over it and took photographs. It was a smaller and more delicate airplane than the Wildcat and it made me feel more confident about the relative qualities of German and American war production. To me bigger was always better. Meanwhile, Chief Revelle couldn't figure out where the second truck came from. He'd only been told about one. It was all too much for him.

* * *

Before 1943 had rolled around, the U.S. Army had come to believe that invasion was no longer a distinct possibility. The German army was bogged down at Stalingrad and General Rommel was heavily engaged in North Africa. Camp was broken at the old school grounds and the troops transferred to the newly expanded Camp Somerset and then later to the European theater. Camp Somerset at Westover became an army installation of considerable consequence and the town, now settling down to the grim realities of the war, did exactly what thousands of other such towns were doing.

I remember the Red Cross offices, located in the little frame building on Broad Street just east of C.H. Hayman's hardware. Miss May Hayman was head of the operation and with the help of a corps of volunteers who apparently took their obligations quite seriously, they produced boxes of pre-prepared bandages and, I suppose, the usual hand-knitted gloves and scarves. It seemed to us as though these ladies were doing something which was much more important than just busy-work. Every volunteer man-hour of labor which the Government could get was one they didn't have to contract out to our already overstressed industry.

Girls in our class, usually concerning themselves with more humanitarian sides of war, could identify with our Red Cross ladies just as we identified with the soldiers. I remember well that Joyce Hickman had committed to memory an old song from the First World War ... *The Rose that Grows in No-Man's Land* ... The chorus ended with a noble, rousing sentiment:

> "...thru' the war's great curse
> stands the Red Cross nurse
> She's the Rose of No-Man's Land"

Soldier's wives by the hundreds came trooping into town, anxious to be with their husbands for those few months while they were awaiting posting overseas. As a way of helping the war effort, we took them in. Spare bedrooms in the great, fine old homes south of Washington Street were rented by the week or month for almost nothing. Ladies whose lives were certainly financially secure, thank you, became land-ladies and mothers-in-absentia for the young girls who poured into town from all over the east coast. We rented the two east bedrooms in our over-large brick home on Washington Street to two young brides and had to turn away many others. They were beautiful young women, closer to my age than my father's and I loved them and they became big sisters to me. Betty Dewey was from Potsdam in up-state New York. From her I learned that not everyone spoke English exactly like an Eastern Shoreman.

We erected a large enclosure in the vacant lot between the Presbyterian Lecture Room and the Fire House for the first aluminum salvage drive. The compound was a dozen feet on each side and draped with red-white-and- blue bunting. Ladies from all over town would drop by with old pots and utensils, and would ask each other for confirmation that their offering was indeed aluminum and not stainless steel.

If you were in elementary school, you'd pick up empty packs of Lucky Strikes and Camels and strip the aluminum foil from the inner wrapper. This you'd roll into a tight little ball and when you found another pack, you'd wrap the new foil around the original ball. Within a few weeks you'd have a fairly commendable ball of pure aluminum and you carried it around in your pocket and rolled it and thumped it on your desk during class until it was a solid and firm, a pure aluminum ingot, a potential rudder or aileron for a P-40 pursuit plane. Mine weighed nearly two pounds and I grew so fond of it that I never turned it in.

Shortages of one kind or another, through never really critical, hounded everybody in town throughout the war. Aluminum was the least of our worries. Then as now, the United States imported much of its raw material and if it came from overseas it was in short supply if you could get it at all.

Rubber was the worst. In the first few weeks of war the Japanese cut off virtually all of our supply when they captured the Dutch East Indies. The news of Pearl Harbor had scarcely left the front page when Washington banned the sale of automobile tires. There were none to be had. Fortunately, my father had just bought one of the last of the 1941 passenger cars and so he began the war with four virtually new tires. He was one of the lucky ones. Many others in town were not.

Put The Lid On The Axis

———————

166 Tons of Scrap Has Been Saved In Somerset For America's Use!

THIS AD SPONSORED BY THE UNDER YOUR SCRAP SIGNED PUBLIC SPIRITED BUSINESSES

Reports of scrap and salvage campaigns of war-critical materials were published regularly in the local newspapers in 1942. Here we see Hitler, Mussolini, and a generic, general-purpose Jap suffering the consequences of Somerset County's patriotic efforts .

Almost immediately, the word came down from Washington that scrap rubber was critical to the war effort. Henry Henderson's Gulf station on main street was designated as a depository for anyone's scrap or unusable tire. I remember a publicity picture in the paper: Mr. E. Mace Smith's daughter, pretty Margaret Ann Smith handing a broadly grinning Carrol Henderson a badly worn six-hundred by sixteen blackwall. Carrol was standing next to a huge wooden pen which was almost full of similar tire carcasses.

If it gained nothing else, that first scrap rubber drive put everyone on an equal footing because shortly thereafter, any used tire, worn or not, would be under Government control and any motorist would treasure it. The War Materials Board soon regulated the sale of every tire in the country, new or used. If, and it was a significant "if", you could prove the need, you'd be permitted to buy a used tire, guaranteed almost as good as any of those being turned in at Henderson's for scrap. A higher need would allow you to purchase a re-treaded (or in some cases, a re-grooved tire which used no new rubber). A truly worthy citizen (a doctor, minister, veterinarian, war worker, or politician) could, upon proper application, buy a new tire if one was available.

All of this was analyzed and adjudicated and fought over by the local Ration Board which set up offices, as I remember, in the Newton Building on Main Street. The Ration Board seemed to arrive in town at about the same time as the soldiers. As the war ground ahead, the Ration Board gradually assumed more and more influence over our lives. The powers of the President and Commissioners of the Town of Princess Anne paled by comparison.

Rationing was a national thing but it wasn't considered unpatriotic to kid and joke about it. Jack Benny and Fred Allen, Eddie Cantor, Bob Hope, and Bing Crosby, all of them used tire jokes in their routines ... the play "Ladies in Retirement" suddenly became "Ladies in Retread-ament" and so on. We laughed. It was all we could do.

Gasoline followed the way of tires in very short order. It wasn't, I believe, that gasoline was in such short supply. We pumped our own crude oil from Oklahoma and Texas. But if you could cut off the gasoline, the tires would last longer. That was the important thing. Within a month, my father lined up at the ration board offices to draw his gas ration book. People fell into three categories: *A, B,* and *X.*

Anybody with a car was entitled to an A card. This provided you with three gallons of gas per week, enough, given the poor milage in those days to get you to the filling station and back. These people accepted their fate and put their cars up on blocks "for the duration" as everyone then called it.

If you were mildly indispensable to the war, a farmer, a merchant, a salesman, or such, you were entitled to a "B" card. This bought you ten gallons of gas per week. My father squeezed out a B Card.

If you were a politician, minister, doctor, or involved directly in war work you drew the coveted "X" card. This was a ticket to a bottomless tank of unlimited gasoline. "What's the worst kind of rival for a guy's girl- friend?" the local jokesters asked. "A 4F-X-er. That's a fellow who's 4-F in the draft with an X-Card in his pocket!"

But the system was hopelessly flawed and it lasted only a few months. With enough X-Cards in Princess Anne, Henry Henderson or Bozman and Hall Esso would fill Dad's tank whenever he needed and they'd charge the gas to the great unaccountable gasoline sump allocated for X-card holders. In short it fell to the honesty of the service station people and to the motorists themselves. And where a man's car was concerned, honesty could often take a back seat to economic need.

Soon even the local newspapers began to editorialize against the X-card. Cars still glutted the roads on Sunday afternoons and Saturday nights would find the parking lots packed at the road houses along Route 13. By early summer, the Government had cracked down on these "pleasure drivers" as we called them. The X-Card was retired and replaced with the C Card. You had to show everyone what your ration status was by putting a printed sticker at the right-hand bottom corner of your windshield, a black A, green B, or a crimson C.

With feelings running high on the subject, it was not wise to leave your car within blocks of the Ocean City boardwalk if you displayed a C-card sticker. My Dad cued up again, this time in the A, B, and C-card sweepstakes. He drew a C-Card based on his work with the wholesale printing industry. Printers and newspapermen marginally made it into the pool of critical jobs. Even though he was limited to 20 gallons a week and could bear the prestigious red "C" sticker on his windshield, it was only marginally enough to see him through his required territory which stretched from Pennsylvania to Virginia.

Gas rationing became an obsession with him. Happiness could almost be equated with the number of gas ration coupons he had in his wallet at any one time. If he couldn't cover his territory properly, we'd be hard-pressed to make ends meet. My father was a gentleman in his bearing, cordial, friendly, affable, but proper. But no one, close friends or acquaintances, could visit us without Dad buttonholing him with one question as they left. "You don't happen to have any spare gas stamps, do you?" It exasperated Mom but she understood, of course.

* * *

My father was an air-raid warden of sorts. Every week he stood an evening's duty at the Princess Anne Public Library on Church Street. There, in an office in the small back room, he'd sit by the telephone. If an air raid alert came, he'd take the ring-down from Salisbury and, somehow, pass the word to the sexton in the Episcopal Church who would then ring a specially coded peal on the church bells which was supposed to alert the town to whatever danger there was. We had several unannounced air-raid drills and the system seemed to work. Nobody thought of calling the telephone a "hot line". It was just the telephone, running through the switchboard at Miss Maude's and on to the Salisbury trunk. Crude as it was, it was not much different from the systems which were at work in rural England at the time.

The big improvement came within a few months when the fire department upgraded their fire siren with a unit which allowed the sounding of a pure, sustained tone like a wail which penetrated to all parts of the town. The Civilian Defense people (we had volunteer offices for almost everything related to the war effort) issued a little chart explaining how the air raid alert would be sounded, what sort of a siren blast would announce an imminent approach of enemy bombers, and how to tell the all-clear blast. It was virtually the same as we used up until the 1960's when people finally realized that we really didn't need fire sirens to alert us to the beginning of a nuclear war.

When an alert sounded, all lights of all kinds were extinguished, the object being to deprive the enemy bombers of a visual bearing on their way to raid Washington. Volunteer air-raid wardens in World War One trench helmets patrolled the streets of town, alert for a stray beam of light from a window. Princess Anne did well. The pilot of an Army observation plane circling over town in May of `42 commended us. We were, he said, a giant pool of inky blackness, distinguishable only by the lights of cars on the road into and out of town.

We also enforced dim-outs as they were called. The dim-out was a permanent every-evening thing which lasted well into the war. Blinds were drawn tightly at dusk, the street lights turned out along Main Street, the Princess Theater darkened, the store windows dimmed, neon signs extinguished. Car headlamps, as of the first of April `42, had to be half-blanked off with a little tar-tape bonnet on their upper half. Later in the summer, we were ordered to blank out the bottom quarter as well, leaving a tiny patch still open, with a usable candle--power only slightly better than a lightning bug. Nobody complained, because with gasoline rationing, not many people were driving anywhere.

I am perhaps among the youngest of those who can well recall a time when horses and buggies were used in Princess Anne for something less glamorous and more practical than Olde Princess Anne Days. I remember that, while Main Street was given to diagonal parking of cars, East Prince William still maintained iron rails for hitching horses. The war and the gasoline shortage revived this phenomenon just as it was dying and gave it a few more years of life. These people weren't trying to be war-time chic like the wealthy ladies who posed in cou-turier overalls in their back-yard Victory gardens. They were poor Somerset farmers, both black and white, from East Princess Anne mostly, who found it easier and cheaper to harness up and come into town for the weekly shopping at Elmer Newton's grocery. The roads to West Post Office were ghastly muddy, gas was short and tires weren't to be had for love nor money. A horse was the answer, obviously.

But war or not, I belonged to the age of the youngster who was born and grew up knowing the automobile. At eight and nine, I and all my friends loved cars, awaited the introduction of the new models in September of each year and lied creatively about the capabilities and speed of whatever make of car our parents owned.

The war changed all of that too. It made cars more precious and more wonderful than ever because there weren't any more new cars, not then, not for the duration. What your parents drove was the car which would, God granting, see them through to that vague time on the distant horizon when the war would be over and all things wonderful would happen again.

The last car, a 1942 Ford sedan, rolled off of the line on the 10th of February, only a bit more than two months after Pearl Harbor, according to official records. And as of New Years Day of that year, sales had been ruthlessly restricted by the Government. Later, cars not already delivered were confiscated by the Government to be doled out to very favored and special people, doctors, ministers, politicians, and the like, naturally. To make it worse, the makers had to fit out each car in so-called black-out trim, which meant applying gray or olive drab paint to all of the chrome and stainless steel trim. As enthusiastic as I was about olive-drab anything, this seemed even to me as a needless desecration.[1]

But the 1942-model cars, with or without blackout trim, were a thing of great status and worthy of almost mystical veneration, and so they remained for four of my most impressionable years. They were bigger than the 1941 models; therefore they too must be better.

Only a few people in town had a genuine 1942 which they bought after the first of January. Not more than a few hundred thousand cars and trucks were available for the whole United States. Dr Whaley got one of them - a 1942 Mercury coupe as I remember. He qualified under the standing Government regulation that you had to have nothing driveable and a legitimate national-interest reason to drive. He applied to the ration board and received a coveted certificate-for-purchase. Given Dr. Whaley's near-legendary reputation for high-speed night-time runs across the salt marshes of Fairmount for which he was duly famous throughout the County, it was not surprising that his year-old 1941Mercury had been reduced to rust and scrap metal.

---

[1] As those of us with enough curiosity later found out, black-out trim had nothing to do with blackouts, as we were told in 1942. It was a well-intentioned effort on the part of the Office of War Production to create a level playing field between those manufacturers who still had a bit of chrome left in stock and those who didn't. Even if you had it, you couldn't flaunt it.

Mr. John B. Roberts was our neighbor on Washington Street. In April of 1942, he came home with the most beautiful dark green Buick Roadmaster I had ever seen. His connection with the paving industry apparently provided his qualifications. Nothing in those days was private; an official notice of his purchase was printed in the local newspaper. Over the course of the war I must have accumulated a goodly number of hours just standing and looking across the street at that car. Somehow he had also managed to avoid the regulation requiring the car delivered in blackout trim. It was pure Detroit chrome and lacquer all the way. Later, when friends would visit me at home, I'd gesture across the street, pointing at that car. "Oh, by the way," I'd say, casually as anything, "That's a `Forty-Two over there," It added, I believed, considerable status to our neighborhood.

Cars were important to all of us. To people of my age, they were things of wonderment, beauty and fascination. To the adults, they were part and parcel of their daily lives. Public transportation in Princess Anne was then precisely what it is today. Nothing. Without automobiles, our local and regional contribution to the war would have come to a stop. No railroads, no poultry, no seafood industry, no lumber, no truck crops, no shipping. I remember standing at Simpkins' Service Station on a cloudy Sunday morning in late `42 or early `43. Next to the north end of the old red garage where Doug or someone had towed it were the remains of a lovely cream-yellow 1939 Buick Century convertible. The front was mashed in and it had partially burned. "That's one less we'll have on the road," I thought. I was truly saddened.

From my father I picked up a certain sixth-sense that a car was an important commodity in the home- front's arsenal in support of the war effort. It was to be cared for and pampered and loved as a member of the family. And it should have been. It was patriotic, we were told. The radio commercial from Cities Service gasoline spoke for us: Drums and a brass band and a military chorus singing *"Care for your car for your Country..."*

Dad took this advice to heart. But country aside, he needed that 1941 Chevrolet. The country's concerns were purely secondary. The best way to keep it running, as he correctly saw it, was with good maintenance and so he became a fanatic on the subject and took it to unbelievable extremes. Every Saturday morning he drove it up to Henry Henderson's Gulf station at the corner of Main and Washington and left it. There they'd drain the oil, lubricate the chassis, grease the latches, and perform any other services which the creative minds of the two Henderson brothers could invent. The car was washed thoroughly and vacuumed. Every month or so, Eddie Gale would Simonize the finish. Little nicks and scratches were immediately touched up. Mid-afternoon he'd pick it up, ready for the to six- to seven-hundred miles he'd put on it the following week.

Over the course of the war, he probably spent more than the initial cost of the car in grease jobs and oil changes, but it was well worth the price. Between October 1941 when he drove it fresh from the showroom of Duncan Brothers Chevrolet just across the bridge in Pocomoke until the distant day in April of 1946 when he passed it on to take delivery on a new Hudson Eight, it performed superbly and never left him stranded. A hundred and forty thousand miles, and the head never was pulled from the engine, he would brag.

The quality and octane of wartime gasoline ranged from poor to terrible and he'd frown and listen to every spark knock. On winter mornings, he'd warm the engine up completely before backing the car out of the garage. He belonged to the school of thought which said that an engine should never be driven until the oil was warm. There was another school of thought which said that idling an engine to warm it up wasted gasoline. Dad belonged to that school too. This dilemma presented him with some rather fundamental conflicts and he agonized over them considerably.

Dad logged enough wartime miles to exceed the factory's predicted actuarial life span of that little Chevrolet coupe by a factor of three, from the Tuscarora Mountains of Pennsylvania to the hot, flat stretches of Route Thirteen down on the Eastern Shore of Virginia. He learned to listen to that car, to understand its secret language and to anticipate its needs. He depended on it and loved it the same way a waterman loves his boat. Its well-being and his and ours were one and the same.

The used-car salesman up in Silver Spring who finally bought it was impressed. New cars were still in short supply in the spring of `forty-six and so he paid Dad something more than $1200, a good $400 more than the car had cost new. He looked at the gleaming black original paint and then at the speedometer, noted the forty-thousand odd miles registering and smiled. He'd found one of those good-quality, low-milage cars which had scarcely been driven since Pearl Harbor. My father also smiled and agreed with him.

* * *

A lot of people in Princess Anne, particularly those unfortunate "A" card holders, turned to bicycles. They weren't rationed or controlled and if you could find one you could buy it. Kids always rode bikes but these weren't kids. Adults formed bike clubs and took five-mile rides on Saturday, health and exercise being considered patriotic. Our teachers at Princess Anne Elementary School rode bikes. At least Julia Ford and some of the other younger teachers did. They were the big, heavy-framed girl's bikes with fat white-wal tires and the kind of big baskets on the handlebars which would flip your front wheel over the wrong way if you overloaded them. Bicycles were everywhere. They were leaned against the front of the A&P and American Store; they were stacked at the corner of Dr. Smith's drug store. We, as youngsters, were the veteran riders. These older people were the novices and the newcomers and the tenderfeet. We viewed them with salty disdain.

The town could have had a more cheerful face and it did by day but at night the dim-out took over. It was fashionable to carry a flashlight and Ever-Ready batteries were not rationed. The Princess Theater blocked the glass panels in its lobby so that out front, by Carey and Carey and Ross's barber shop, the dark and gloom made you look hard to identify a friend coming out of the movies. The dim-outs continued almost through the end of the war.

This was not foolishness and indeed it was perhaps our most significant contribution to the war effort. Submarine warfare was not a threat, it was a deadly reality with ships burning within sight of Ocean City and Rehobeth and people took it very seriously. Ships leaving Norfolk in convoy would have been silhouetted clearly against the sky glow from the homes on the Eastern Shore as they made their way to join with other trans-Atlantic convoys forming up in New York and Halifax.

The submarine threat brought the war home closely to all of us. We heard tales of bodies being washed ashore from Henlopen to Hatteras. Parts of Ocean City's main beach were unusable in August of `42 because of the quantity of crude oil drifting ashore, spilled from tankers which now lay on the bottom less than a dozen miles out. I recall fishing in Tangier Sound that summer with family on a boat piloted by Captain Roland Bozman of Wenona. A side of beef from a locker of a sunken ship had drifted up on the tide from Cape Henry Virginia.

Meat, of course, was rationed and unless you were a farmer or knew one, beef was hard to come by and when you got it, it was, as we said, "ditch-bank" beef, stringy and tough and lean. But here was a prime side of beef, floating within grappling hook distance. Captain Roland looked at the beef, then at my father, then back at the beef.

"What do you think, Frank? Should we haul her aboard?"

"I don't know. You think it's still good?"

"Looks good to me. `Course you can't tell how long she's been floatin' and what she's been through."

They discussed, argued, and worried. It was more meat than we'd get from Elmer Newton's store for a year if we went by our ration tokens. My father, being prudent, finally decided against it. Captain Roland, didn't really want to risk it anyhow, and so he kicked over the old marine one-lunger and we chugged away, leaving a half a beef bobbing on the surface of Tangier Sound, half way between Wenona and Rumbley.

That summer gave rise to nasty rumors and hard words within the town. At least one Somerset County resident was openly accused of secretly selling diesel fuel to German U-boats operating off of our ocean beaches. We had, purportedly, good reason to suspect the man. Nominally a farmer, he spent most of his time operating a "bucket-of-blood" road house just south of King's Creek, the sort of place which was off-limits to our soldiers at Camp Somerset. But as a farmer, he had laid in vast quantities of fuel oil in tanks on his farm, much more, people said, than that needed to operate his tractor. Then too, he had money, much more than he'd ever had before. That the man was probably black-marketing diesel oil and gasoline never occurred to any of us, and that he was making a small fortune from the after-hours sale of liquor was ignored. The story was too good. We heard that the FBI was looking into the matter. We hoped that they would charge him with espionage and treason and we could all go to the hanging.

As a conclusion to what would otherwise have been a mystery, I chanced, only recently, to become friends with a German navy petty-officer who sailed in one of those U-boats, the U-373. His route, he told me laughing, was from Cape Henry to the Ben Franklin Bridge in Philadelphia and by mid-42 he'd already made three patrols to our coast.

"Fred," I asked him once. "I have something serious to ask you and I want you to give me an honest answer." I told him my story. "Did you," I asked, "ever load diesel fuel from the Eastern Shore, like down around Chincoteague?"

"No," he said. "We had plenty of fuel oil for the patrol. Our problem was with potable water. Now if he'd been out there selling fifty-five gallon drums of drinking water, we might have done some business." Those of us who still remember the stories about this purported traitor which were making the rounds back then may as well lay the subject to rest. A profiteer yes, traitor no. I know. I got it from the horse's mouth, so to speak.

* * *

Our ration board stayed busy. As the war news got better, rationing became worse. The ration board finally got full wind in its sails and began to move with imposing majesty. Early in the war it took its basic training on easy things like tires and gasoline. Later as it became more skilled, it expanded its line of rationed items to include all manner of daily staples and by late 1942 and 1943 we were rationing shoes, meat, canned goods, coffee, butter and sugar. This meant ration books for everybody and to make change, little dime-sized red and blue plastic ration tokens.

Food isn't an easy thing to ration and the Government allowed all kinds of exemptions and loop-holes. If you saved fat and grease from your bacon until you had a one-pound coffee can full of the stuff you could haul it to the ration board or a grocery store or somewhere and they'd give you a handful of the little red meat-ration tokens. Saving fat was considered to be a high order of patriotic gesture, even if you didn't need the tokens.

Meat substitutes were the thing. The cheese people selflessly conceived of the idea for Meatless Tuesdays. The Franco-American spaghetti people were always on hand to tell us of another great new patriotic meat-substitute recipe which would help win the war a little faster. Mother served macaroni and cheese with a little crumbled bacon topping and it became my favorite.

Sugar was one of our first staples to be rationed, mostly because our principal supplies came from Cuba and merchant shipping was diverted to Atlantic convoy duty. You had to declare the number of pounds of sugar you had on hand at the outset of rationing, with the implication being that falsification of your sugar inventory report was a crime less than treason but not much.

Dad braved it. He wasn't hoarding sugar. (Hoarding was a word applied then with much the same official contempt as "drug-smuggling" is today.) He just so happened to have a lot on hand when the war started. It was cleverly buried in a box down by the coal pile in our basement, two or three yellow five-pound bags of pure Domino Cane. I believe that Dad felt mildly disappointed because nobody ever came around to inspect.

You could also draw extra sugar if you were canning although how this was determined escapes me at present. Nevertheless I feel sure that many independent businessmen engaged in moonshine operations back in Pocomoke Swamp took advantage of this loophole to obtain a little more sugar for the mash.

Coffee was rationed and in short supply and people in town divided themselves roughly into two camps: those who cut down on the coffee grounds which went into the pot, and those who insisted that they'd rather have one good cup than a dozen cups of that darned dish-water. Mom was in the former group but the mothers of some of my best friends were adherents to the latter philosophy.

The ration board also gave out coupons for shoes although growing people of my age were exempt, unless we insisted on leather shoes. A lot of us wore unrationed Keds but the treaded rubber soles were gradually replaced with some sort of a gummy yellow foam sponge which soaked up water when we got them wet.

Much which wasn't rationed was in short supply. Dad's favorite cigarettes, Chesterfields, weren't always available in the stores. Vast quantities of all of the name-brand cigarettes were diverted to the Armed Forces and every pre-packaged field ration carried three or four foil-wrapped cigarettes. In their place, the Home Front was introduced to strange new brands which nobody had heard of before and mercifully no one heard of after the war. Cartons of *Wings*, with airplane trading cards stuck to the back of each pack, were bought in quantity only because they were reasonably plentiful. I collected Wings cards and rejoiced when Dad couldn't find Chesterfields at Dougherty and Hayman's.

Beer was available and the Dispensary carried enough Schenley's blended whiskey and Four Roses but good   Scotch was only a memory and a fifth of excellent Bourbon was a prize to be cherished above all others. We were led to believe that somehow the were supporting the war effort but just how was never made clear.[2]

In early 1943, toothpaste went too. Because toothpaste tubes contained aluminum, Pepsodent and Ipana went off to war and in their places we were introduced to cardboard boxes of tooth powder and bottles of a sticky-sweet red- or blue-colored syrup dubbed as a "liquid

---

[2] Distilleries produced alcohol for the production of explosives and were legitimately a part of the war effort. This simple and reasonable explanation was never afforded to us, on the basis that it was "sensitive" information.

dentifrice" My box of tooth-powder never had a shelf life long enough to use it all up. Half way through the box, the cardboard would disintegrate under the normal splash of water. Of the two I remember developing a secret, somewhat guilt-ridden preference for the liquid stuff. It foamed a lot and tasted almost good and didn't feel like sand in your mouth the way that tooth-powder did. This told me that it probably wasn't really doing a good job, but I kept my feelings to myself.

Actually, rationing and occasional shortages were sort of fun and most people secretly enjoyed them because it made everybody feel like they were giving up something important for the war effort. But we weren't really. Anyone alive in Eastern Europe in 1980 would gladly swap their whole state-controlled store system for the amazing quantity and quality of goods which were available to us in 1943 under these, the most severe of wartime rationing conditions.

* * *

As the war drew on, it became more remote, less immediate to me than those days with the 29th Division in town. The war was now a day-to--day businesslike operation. The shipyards up at Sparrow's Point in Baltimore were turning out Liberty Ships and scores of Eastern Shore craftsmen and carpenters and welders became Western Shoreman for the Duration. Graduation from Washington High School was almost always followed by a notice from a fellow's draft board. The white silk Service Flag which the Presbyterian Church displayed up by the pulpit grew longer and longer, with a symbollic blue star on a white field for every service man from Princess Anne. A few of the blue stars turned to gold over the course of 1943 as the fighting and killings intensified.

I was no longer ten, but eleven and then twelve. Some things don't become a twelve-year old boy, at least in his own mind. A twelve-year old just doesn't go running, screaming into the street every time a six-wheeler army truck loaded with soldiers passes. It was much more worldly to be self-contained, perhaps a little blasé.

There were compensations to be sure, the great, spectacular military bands for one thing. Before the war the only honestly live music I'd ever heard performed was at the firemen's carnival over on Beechwood Street where Happy Johnny and His Boys would bring their hillbilly band down from Baltimore to keep the crowds spending nickels and dimes for an extra hour on Saturday evening. But the war broadened my outlook considerably.

On a Sunday afternoon, an Army brass band on its way from somewhere to some place else would de-bus itself up on Main Street and march smartly to the Courthouse steps and provide everybody with as much Sousa as they could easily take aboard. War bond sales, I am sure, had something to do with their presence.

They were full-ranked bands, with conductor and rows of clarinets and peck horns and oboes and coronets. They carried new and shiny and undented instruments, unlike those which were the sole remnants of the old pre-war firemen's band and which were stored casually in the back upstairs room of the firehouse.

And they were loud. I'd slip up on the porch of the court house, behind the musicians to get a better view of the instruments and music and there I'd wait for that first note in full glory and maximum volume. It was a while later before I learned of the subtle and delicate beauties of music played pianissimo. I was quite sure that our boys could play louder than any German military band of equal size.

And there was that great time in the summer of `forty-three when the Army went south on maneuvers and thoughtfully brought all of their trash back home with them and then dropped it in the marsh just down from Red Bridge on the Deal Island Road. It was a veritable mountain of trash which you could wade out to and then climb up on. There were notebooks full of expired battle orders and expended paper cartridges, red and blue guidon battle flags, and canteens with holes in them, and used mess kits. I can still remember wading knee-deep in that trove of military treasure, the unforgettable smell of stale cordite mingling with that particular smell of the Manokin River on a hot August afternoon. I never found anything worth bringing home, most likely because I was older and more discerning than I once had been. But I looked hard, for it seemed that the ultimate treasure just had to be out there somewhere just beyond my reach on the next mudflat.

The Great Military Dump was probably an ecological disaster by anybody's reckoning, and it's hard to imagine such a thing happening in today's climate of Environmental Impact Statements and Wetlands concerns. And it would be of all the greater concern were it known that children were splowing around in the middle of this great mound of soggy paper, jagged metal, chemical waste, and war's general impedimenta and detritus, all partially submerged in the questionable waters of the old Manokin.

The Mountain remained through the declining days of the war, growing smaller and more homogenous as the months wore on. The cartridges and papers and ammunition boxes met their final destinies as a part of the landfill at the southwest intersection of Route 13 and the Deal Island Road when they built the new highway in the 1960's. I never found anything worthwhile in the whole deposit when it was brand-spanking new. I doubt if future archeologists will either.

I tried hard that summer to keep the spirit alive, but to all of us, the war was no longer new and exciting and breathtaking. It had become heavy and ponderous and all-consuming and all-pervasive. We were going to win. We knew it. We just wanted to get on with it and get it over with.

In the seventh grade of an afternoon, we'd go corner a booth in Elmer Jones' Restaurant up on Main Street. We spoke quietly among ourselves, of course, because Jones' at that time was the undisputed preserve of the high school students. They suffered us to stay there so long as we remembered our places and behaved ourselves.

Anne Whaley and Reds Smith and Denny Bloodsworth, Laura Catherine Jones and Martha Lee Thompson and others, all the cream of Washington High School Society, would hold forth at Elmer Jones', drinking Cokes and eating Lance cheese crackers and feeding nickels to the juke box to hear the Andrews Sisters sing *Drinkin' Rum and Coca Cola*. On occasions they'd buy cigarettes, not packs like anybody else, but lone cigarettes at a penny a piece from already opened packs. The girls, particularly, looked terribly sophisticated. On other occasions, a sailor, looking trim in tailored dress blues and Pea-coat would come in for a milk-shake and there'd be a general shuffling and tittering and disorder from the booths where the girls sat.

I remember sitting in a front booth one rainy afternoon. The new copy of *Life* had come in. It bore the cover photograph which, even by today's candid, no-holds-barred standards, stands starkly in the memory of journalism professors as a watershed of graphic wartime photo-realism. I can still see it in my mind, a riveting close-up of the head of a Japanese soldier, severed, burned, and impaled on the superstructure of a U.S. tank somewhere on a Pacific atoll.

We had a copy and we sat there casting glances at it, trying our hardest to be nonchalant and not sick to our stomachs. To show revulsion would be to show a lack of spirit. *C'est la Guerre*, we would have said with a shrug if we'd been in first-year French and had known the word. "Only one thing wrong with it," someone said. I believe it was Francis Panzer. "There ought to be a thousand of them instead of just that one." "He sure as hell died for his Emperor," somebody else laughed.

We were starting to win, now and we felt cocky. It wouldn't be to-morrow, but, well, sometime. Every magazine advertisement promised us eventual victory. "Di-di-di-dah", Morse code for "V" which stood for Victory, was the standard way of honking a horn if you drove a truck on Route 13. There'd be more Jap casualties, just like that one on the cover of *Life*. More Sons of the Rising Sun would go forth to join their Ancestors. We looked forward to it.

The news that we'd recount to ourselves after school seemed to get better week by week just as I'd always felt that it would. History, it seemed, was always on the side of the optimist, particularly if you lived in the United States. We'd carried out the successful invasion of North Africa back in `42. And on a May morning in 1943, I took a copy of the *Baltimore Sun* down to the river bank with me and sat there and watched the Manokin in that clean, sparkling spring air and read, for the first time, the place-names of Tunis and Bizarte and watched the black areas of the North African war map become smaller and smaller with each day's paper. The feared *Afrikakorps* of General Erwin Rommel was surrendering in wholesale numbers to American boys and I was incredibly proud of my country and its army. American Eighth Air

Force bombers from England were striking heavily at Germany's North Sea ports and Ruhr valley.

And as our successes multiplied overseas, patriotism at home reached joyful levels of enthusiasm. By some sort of mutual consent, every magazine publisher in the United States set aside the month of July in 1943 to display the American Flag on its cover. Even the staid old *National Geographic* broke with tradition and forsook its traditional yellow, lettered cover for one with a demure, modest portrayal of Old Glory. The magazine racks in Carey's were ablaze with red-white-and-blue during that one month. I set forth to collect as many magazines as possible and carefully cut each flag out and put them all in a folder. My grandmother, handy at such things, took the whole batch and colorfully shellacked them to an old wooden tub which she used for potted plants. The display of patriotism, it seemed, had even reached to her level.

We anticipated D-Day, the eventual invasion of France, I perhaps more than many of the adults who could remember the terrible casualties which trench warfare of the First World War inflicted on the poor soldiers of both sides. But in my mind, the rationale was simple: We won the first War because we had long lines of trenches stretched across the mid-section of France. Victory would again be ours just as soon as we could get troops ashore in France, have Paris to our rear and the Rhine to our front. From our library, I took out and studied huge old leather-bound volumes about that War and read them on the living room floor until I had committed all of those great successful battles to heart and could show you the location of the Argonne and Ypres in my sleep. If only we could get on with it, just like it was, with hundreds of thousands of GI's reverting to dough-boys, supported by millions of cheering, grateful Frenchmen, we could all sing *Mam'selle from Armentieres* and the war would soon be over.

But for us in Princess Anne, Chincoteague's Naval Air Station provided plenty of military interest in the skies. Chincoteague was the site of a patrol bomber base, hurriedly constructed to meet the challenge of the Battle of the Atlantic. And while victory was not yet come, the big Consolidated four-engine, land-based patrol bombers made it difficult for the U-Boats still brave enough to lie out off of Ocean City.

Chincoteague was a major air base for the Navy and in addition to the patrol bombers, they carried out training missions as well as a wide range of general military aviation support duties.

Grumman *Avengers*, a particularly lethal-appearing single-engine torpedo bomber, flew in tight formation, six and seven abreast, impressive in their sky-blue and gray camouflage. At least once a day, usually at dinner time, a single flight would come roaring up Route 13 and over Princess Anne at the thousand-foot minimum or lower, shaking the windows and vibrating the earth with the sheer power of their huge radial engines. I'd wait at the table until I could stand it no longer and then I'd take off scrambling for the back yard to see them. Once an entire squadron from Philadelphia made a massed run down the Shore to Chincoteague. The noise was far away when I first heard them, but big and expansive and awe-inspiring and within minutes the sky was full of them. I counted twenty or thirty and there were more that got away.

* * *

In mid-summer of 1943, I joined Troop 145 of the Boy Scouts of America. In Wartime Princess Anne, this wasn't exactly a volunteer act. A young boy in hiking distance of the Scout House at Church and Broad Streets joined because he was quite expected to join. Not to have done so would have revealed some character flaw, perhaps lack of patriotism. It was the junior equivalent of the draft.

Scouting of that period had little to do with the sociologically oriented program which passes for Scouting today. With the exception of rudimentary Woodsmanship and an occasional honorific Scout salute to Lord Baden-Powell, it was quasi-military all the way. John Jefferies was my scoutmaster and he was assisted by at least one volunteer infantry sergeant from Camp Somerset. We had a military organization, two patrols with senior scouts of various ranks at the upper echelons. The Army sergeant was in charge of drills and inspections. My strongest memories of that time are not of the proper tieing of the bowline knot, but of mastering the footwork of an about-face in a proper military manner.

We'd line up in Broad Street, a dozen or so to a patrol, surveilled at first by Patrol Leaders Sandy Jones or Reds Smith and then, when they were satisfied, by the Sergeant himself. He was a no-nonsense fellow who never smiled much and tolerated not so much as an inch of misalignment in the squad's dress order. We stood, campaign hats squared and neckerchiefs properly tied. Nobody complained. That's just the way things were expected to be done in the Scouts, we assumed.

Later, when my time came in the Korean War and I stood sweating in a Pensacola Naval Aviation Cadet formation in flight training with a Marine non-com drill instructor staring me down Officer-and-Gentleman style, it held no real fear for me. I'd been through it all before. And back there with Troop 145, it had been every bit as tough, every bit as demanding as it was under the Florida sun. I knew my close-order drill. I knew how to march already. I'd been well taught back in Princess Anne by the U.S. Army while still in the Boy Scouts.

Scouting played a big part in our lives as we went from sixth to seventh grade. Work and advancement was expected. Senior men in town sat on our Boards of Review to ensure that we'd mastered the expected material, Mr. Everett Cannon for electricity, Arthur Powell for business practices and bookkeeping. They took it seriously and therefore so did we.

Hans Christian Schilling, the most formidable, and most high-ranking Scout leader on the Shore, so far as we could tell, came early in 1944 to inspect our troop. Mr. Schilling was physically one of the most imposing men I ever saw, big as William Bendix, handsome, sandy haired, with a thick German accent and a manner which placed him half way between a neurotic Prussian drill sergeant and Pat O'Brien deepinto his Father Flannigan role.

I stood his inspection that winter night in a haze of such terror and worry that I scarcely remember the end of it, but Troop 145 came through to the point where he didn't publicly rip off our merit badges and drum us out of the Corps. He was from Salisbury, a goldsmith by trade and an immigrant who, he told us later in the evening, had come from Stuttgart, Germany in 1923, the year of their terrible inflation.

He and his wife were destitute with no food and a room full of worthless money. On one particular day, life seemed so hopeless that both had resolved to take their own lives rather than starve to death in their apartment. But, as he told us after the inspection, there were things to do first. The mail, for example, must be brought in. It was then that he found the letter from Philadelphia which bore his name. Inside was a single American dollar bill. No note. No return address. He never found out who sent it or why.

But it was a turning point for the Schillings. They resolved to go to America and so they did, settling in this country, eventually moving to Salisbury and finding success. Hard work and dedication seemed to be his watchword. After his inspection (perhaps because of it) our mission seemed to change. There was a war on and there was hard work to be done. The Boy Scouts in those days was a working organization.

It involved scrap and salvage. The scrap paper collection was handed over to the Boy Scouts as well as bits and pieces of other scrap and salvage collections. It was a formidable task and one that never ended. On a Saturday, we'd pile on the back of an open stake-bed truck and make the drive through Oriole or Dame's Quarter or perhaps Fairmount and Frenchtown, stopping every hundred yards to jump off and hoist an arm-load of soggy newspapers or magazines aboard. Then when we were good and tired out so that we couldn't move anymore, we'd have to take them back to Princess Anne and unload everything in a corrugated steel shed on Church Street next to the old library.

If that was all, it might have been fun of sorts. But the scrap dealer up by the railroad tracks in Fruitland insisted that scrap papers needed to be bundled just so. On our own time, we'd go around to that dank shed, smelling of rotting, moldering newsprint and bale, using roll upon roll of binder twine. It wasn't the sort of job that had an end, for as we sent bales to Fruitland, we brought more raw papers in. It was the sort of job which had a way of making you feel bad about yourself because whenever you had a few minutes to do something you wanted to do, you'd feel guilty because you weren't bundling papers.

It was a never-ending job. If the war hadn't ended, I harbor a secret fear that I'd be there yet today. I was in that open Chevy stake-body truck waist-deep in paper with Adrian and George Bozman, George Miles, Jack Keller, and Ralph Dryden on our way to Fruitland on the 5th of May 1945 when the word came that the war in Europe was over. Perhaps by directive, perhaps by mutual disgust, we unloaded that truck and never returned to the job of paper salvage again. We'd help win the war in Europe and that was enough. The Pacific war would just have to make do without us.

* * *

In late 1943, Camp Somerset's soldiers were finally withdrawn and relocated at Fort Story and Hampton Roads Virginia where most of them went on to participate in the D-Day invasion. Camp Somerset itself became a prisoner-of-war camp for German soldiers who were caught up in the collapse of their armies in North Africa in the spring of 1943. Major Arthur Eaker of Muncy Pennsylvania, became one of its commandants and I spent many happy days and evenings at Camp Somerset as a guest of his youngest daughter. It was there that I realized that German troops really weren't much different from the boys in the 29th Division. Both, in retrospect, looked homesick.

They came in by the hundreds in troop trains which unloaded at the siding in Westover. They were strong, sturdy, sunburned veterans of the *Afrikakorps*, generally disillusioned at the war and really angry only at their Italian allies. Almost immediately they were sent out into the farms and orchards and canning houses on a volunteer basis to help with the harvests. They were respected and tolerated by most of the people and genuinely liked by more than a few. They fitted in well and seemed to enjoy themselves greatly. A few well-meaning farmers assumed that if a boy worked hard in the field for six days a week, it just might be good manners to have him back on the seventh for Sunday dinner. This practice wasn't condoned by Major Eaker or the rest of the U.S. Army, so far as I knew. But it continued. I think the farmers just felt they didn't need to make much of an issue of it.

Ironically, it was those German soldiers rather than the fresh young recruits of the Twenty-ninth who came to Princess Anne's rescue in time of disaster. Early in September of 1944, a major hurricane struck the Eastern Shore. Trees were uprooted, power lines went down, and the town was concerned with the possibility of losing its water supply because of the joint dangers of flooding and the lack of electricity. The war made things doubly difficult. Men weren't available to man the clean-up crews. Back then, hurricanes weren't given cute names like Hazel and Alice. This one was, in the local description, "one hell of a big blow!"

My grandmother who at the time was President of Commissioners in town made some sort of arrangement with Major Eaker and within a day a truckload of German soldiers reported for duty, shovels and crosscut saws at the ready. A unit was detached to clear limbs from Beckford Avenue.

Jack Keller was standing by his house at the corner of Linden and Beckford watching the work progress. Three or four prisoners were hard at work and the day was growing warm. The guard seemed indifferent. As Jack watched, one huge blond prisoner edged away from the group and walked silently over to where he stood. To Jack, this ex-enemy looked as big as Attila the Hun and was probably a crazed, fanatical Nazi to boot.

He was petrified with fear. After years of hating these people in the abstract, he now found himself face-to-face with one. And the guard paid no heed, seeming not to care one bit if this prisoner broke off, established his own local branch of the Third Reich in Princess Anne and made a poor little local boy its first victim.

"Wasser" the big man said, staring down at Jack. Jack spoke not a word of German. He was still courageously battling the French language, but somehow the meaning came through. Jack turned and ran for his kitchen, grabbed a glass and poured a big glass of "Wasser" and started for the door. Thinking better of it, he stopped, pulled a tray of ice from the refrigerator, dumped it into a pitcher and filled it to the brim. For good measure, he put it on a tray with a fresh glass. He wanted it to look good. Maybe this man would spare his life.

It wasn't much of an adventure. The POW drank it down, smiled and probably said "Danke" as he'd been taught. Jack was allowed to go free.

A dozen or more from another group reported to the Presbyterian churchyard with an Army Private in tow as guard, and I remember spending an afternoon with them there. With me that day was my other Grandmother, Marie Pierce, who lived in Washington and who visited us once or twice each year on delightful flying visits filled with laughter, presents and fun.

She was German, from a Washington family straight out of the *Schwarzwald* part of Southern Germany when they came to the United States in the 1880's. She walked quietly among the dozen or so prisoners, her ears sharp to their scatterings of conversation, a smug smile on her face. Little old ladies in Princes Anne who spoke perfect German were not a common commodity and she knew it.

Two fellows pumped a cross-cut saw and the work was hard and the afternoon long. "*Wie spät ist es?*"(What time is it?), one asked. The other shrugged his shoulders and answered his friend in German, "I don't know. I'll ask the old woman there," he said.

Now there are ways, in German, to refer politely to an elderly lady but the term he used, "*Alte Weib*" is not one of the complimentary ones, not at all. It translates best as "old bat". And my Grandmother, of course, had heard and understood all. She answered him not in perfect German but, as she told me laughing over dinner that night, "but in a good thick Bavarian dialect, just like he spoke at home. Smart little puppy," she added. "His momma would be shocked."

They worked hard that day. They were a relaxed and good-humored lot and that guard didn't fear that they'd bolt and run either. He just sat in the shade of the old sycamore tree which used to stand there in the churchyard. They didn't want to escape. At the end of each day they climbed properly into the truck back to Westover. The Eastern Shore was a good place to sit out any war. These soldiers knew it.

* * *

A presidential election came in November of 1944. It was a strange election, getting lost in the war news of the U.S. Army's triumphant march across Occupied France. Far from the student involvement in today's elections, those of us in the Freshman class at Washington High School paid it precious little heed.

The outcome was considered foregone. We had a mock polling place set up in the front corridor as I remember it, and Franklin Roosevelt won handily, defeating Republican Thomas E. Dewey of New York even more roundly than he did in the real elections a few weeks later. Eastern Shoremen at that time were a part of the Solid South which meant you'd vote Democratic, come what may.

Two or three of us were Dewey supporters, Ted Phoebus was, but that hardly counted because his father was a staunch Republican. So were Jack Keller and Pat White. I voted for Dewey that morning not out of any loyalty to the Grand Old Party but because everyone I heard seemed to resent the wartime bureaucracy which Washington ladened upon us. It was a protest vote, before the term became popular.

The Democrats had a slogan and a pretty effective one it was: "Don't change horses in the middle of the stream" My grandfather, a died-in-the-wool Democrat since he cast his first vote for Tilden back in 1876, grumbled constantly about Roosevelt and the New Dealers as he called them. "If I couldn't get him out of the middle of that stream," he'd fume, "I'd shoot the dod-rotted horse!"

But he didn't. As he'd done all of his life, and like most of Princess Anne, he walked uptown to the polling place on Beechwood Street and he voted for Roosevelt. And Roosevelt, tired and sick and enfeebled, went off to Yalta to deal with Joe Stalin and to carve up and parcel out all of post-war Eastern Europe. But we didn't understand long-term things like that. He was our President and it would be, well, unpatriotic not to vote for him. Don't change horses.

* * *

I wasn't in Princess Anne when the Bomb was dropped on Hiroshima. I regret it that I wasn't. I was in Washington DC. I wish I could have walked up to Carey and Carey's and had a coke and generally felt good about everything while we all told each other that we knew it would all come out all right anyhow.

44

There was a party of sorts that evening at my uncle's house at Oxen Hill in Upper Marlboro in the southern outskirts of Washington. The adults were full of victory and confidence and the last of the pre-war Bourbon. "It's all over now but the shoutin'," they told each other over and over.

But my uncle wasn't given to over-optimism. He told me not to assume too much. The war wasn't over, he opined, and so far as he could tell from the radio, this thing was just a big fire bomb. But it wasn't. I told him I'd read all about it in a comic book back in 1944. It told how we were going to split the atom and use it in a bomb and I knew exactly what this bomb was. I was on the money. Much to the concern of the Manhattan Project people and the FBI and heavens-knows how many other Washington agencies, an enterprising comic-book writer had independently doped out the basic concepts and laid it all out for everybody. He'd dropped his into the crater of Mount Fuji and had destroyed Tokyo in cataclysmic earthquakes but the results were the same. The effect of his fiction on official security-obsessed Washington was less than the fictional earthquakes, but not significantly less. Fiction it was, but the principle was there in full color. Much of what all of us thought we knew about the war came from comic books, of course. And so it was somehow fitting that a comic book transitioned me away from the days of iron bombs and massed infantry and into the Nuclear Age.

But my uncle was right. The war wasn't over. It ground on for another week while we obliterated Nagasaki and the Russians conveniently declared war on Japan and overran half of our late enemy's Asian land empire. President Truman cautioned against premature celebrations. My visit at an end, I came back to Princess Anne.

The war ended for me a few evenings later, on an unforgettable warm August night in 1945. It ended in celebration just as it did for so many others around the world. "The Allies are victorious on land, sea, and in the air," President Truman told us, his mid-western nasal voice coming out over the speakers of millions of radios.

It was all over. Not a ship would weigh anchor anywhere across the mighty expanse of the Pacific basin without the express permission of the United States Navy. That night witnessed the absolute pinnacle of America's power, a time which likely as not we'll never see again. We had won and the forty-five wartime months since Pearl Harbor had marked me just as it permanently marked everyone, adult or child, who lived through that time. It just marked some of us more quietly than others.

The great Post-War World, for which we had worked and prayed and yearned was at last at hand. It was official. We could celebrate. Princess Anne brought out its two fire engines, the new 1940 American La France and the old open 1927 La France pumper. We paraded around the streets, up Beckford and down Beechwood. A girl whom I knew from her visits to Princess Anne from summers past was wildly and flamboyantly kissing a sailor from Chincoteague as she clung to the back of the old pumper, one arm gripping the brass rail and the other around his neck, just like in the movies.

She was always so delicate, so shy, I thought. She was the slender, intense little girl with pale hands and thick dark braids who used to sit with us during the heat of the day on her front porch and we'd drink lemonade and she'd shape little doll figures out of hollyhock blossoms and make up remarkable, fanciful stories for her two little sisters. This wasn't like her. Not at all. And then I understood.

She was growing up, of course. And so was I.

————————————

I remember - The Firemen's Carnivals

Before his death a few years ago, Mr. Bob Jones would write an occasional column for the local Princess Anne newspaper. Bob was born back at the turn of the Century and his recollections went back a lot further than my own. Because I am sure I love that town considerably more now, having left it, than perhaps I ever did in my days of growing up there, I was a frequent and involved reader of Bob Jones' informal little nostalgia column, *Down Memory Lane*, which appeared with some regularity in the local *Marylander and Herald* newspaper. Bob had often spoken of his house back on Beechwood Street at Irving Avenue, the one which burned down long ago, years before I was born. Bob was of an earlier generation than I, so I don't remember the house, but I well remember the stone steps which must have led to his front porch. When I was very young, those two steps were the only man-made artifact blemishing what was, by my accounts, the best pair of vacant lots in town.

For the better part of the year, they afforded me convenient open ground for running, wrestling, screaming, and getting dirty. But for two or three weeks every summer, those two lots became the literal polar center of my young world. For it was on these very grounds that the Princess Anne Volunteer Fire Department staged its annual Firemen's Carnival.

The Carnival meant excitement of the most exotic kind, evenings and nights of color, music, crowds, games, noise, and adventure. From Monday evening through Saturday night for two whole weeks, the Firemens' Carnival was the cultural and social capital of Princess Anne. Nobody within the corporate town limits and few within the entire northern county could escape its influence.

The actual date would vary but the big event generally fell the last two weeks in July, give or take a week or so. It was a time to rejoice. By then we had detonated the last of the Fourth of July's firecrackers, Pine Beach and Sandy Hill Beach up on the Wicomico were full of stinging nettles, and we'd already had the Presbyterian Sunday School Picnic at

Ocean City. So without the Carnival, school summer vacation could have lain heavy on our hands.

Like a train still faraway down the tracks, the approaching presence of the Carnival could be felt and heard long before you could see it. Long weeks ahead, I'd know of its coming. Pre-printed multi-colored lithographed posters would be over-printed at the Marylander and Herald offices with the official dates. Huge shipping boxes full of stuffed animals imaginatively tinted in purples and violets and crates of equally resplendent china figurines would arrive at the Fire Department. Committee appointments would be made among the firemen and I, keeping an ear and an eye always open for such things, was generally among the first to know.

At first hearing, I'd run to the great vacant lot, searching for some concrete evidence of the coming. But there'd be none, nothing to break the bleak expanse of hot dead yellow grasses and the perennial hollyhock stalks along the fence at Miss Janie Wilson's property. I'd reconcile myself but the excitement had already begun.

We lived directly across the street in the big brick house at the corner of Washington and Beechwood so the area was almost like my own back yard. Every morning after breakfast I'd run to the vacant lot to see if anything had sprung up over night, rather like I do today on the morning after I plant the lettuce in the spring. When, after days of waiting, the first evidence finally arrived, it was always a little dispiriting, probably nothing more than a truck load of rough pine lumber, two-by-fours and one-by-sixes from Cohn and Bock's lumber company.

But plain as it was, it was symbolic of things yet to come and it was always good for fifteen or twenty minutes of intense examination and an additional hour of daydreaming. But once delivered, the lumber would sit there in the sun and rain, curing and warping, untouched. I'd check it carefully every morning and woefully not a stick would be out of place. No construction site in the 1990's could ever remain so untouched and unstolen for so long.

48

The firemen had it well planned out. A week or so before opening date, a crew of a dozen-odd volunteers would appear, generally headed by Mr. Walter McDowell. A muscular, stooped, and dour old gentleman with white hair and well trimmed mustache, he had not much time for small talk. Walter McDowell was a senior carpenter in town and one of the earliest members of the fire department. The layout of the lot was not a casual thing, as I see it now. It must have taken a lot of planning. Mr. McDowell had plans drawn which designated the position of everything on the grounds down to the last square foot and he and his crew were responsible for making everything fit.

At the first cutting of wood, I was on hand, early morning until late, watching, trying to stay out of the way, but it was grand. A half-dozen or more small exhibition booths needed to be constructed, open-fronted, probably eight by twelve feet on the average each with a sloping roof, and perhaps two windows on the sides for ventilation. But the major engineering effort was the bandstand, a huge platform of a couple of hundred or more square feet, elevated off the ground, railed above and structured and stressed and trussed below with massive two-by-ten beams. No effort was spared. This was the nerve center of the carnival.

When Mr. McDowell and his crew got around to starting the construction of the bandstand, we all knew that the carnival was finally at hand. Planning and ordering and placarding with signs were all in the past. Time zero had arrived from which the next two or three weeks would be measured. Everybody of school age on Beechwood street arrived early and stayed until late or until run off home by a fireman.

* * *

An affair as grand as a firemen's carnival could never be properly staged by volunteer firemen alone. It required highly specialized professional help. Fortunately for Princess Anne and other small towns like it, professional help was available in the form of itinerant carnival troupes. On Wednesday or Thursday before the great opening, one of these troupes would arrive in town and take up station on the carnival grounds. If the erecting of the bandstand was the beginning of phase one, the arrival of the carny workers on the grounds was the beginning of the second great epoch.

The carnival people could galvanize a small boy's attention by their sheer presence. They weren't Princess Anne folks and you could tell it right away. You could live and play and wander throughout the town for a year and never see anyone quite their equal for rough appearance, colorful swearing, and casual outlook on life.

They'd arrive in a caravan, not a circus caravan with all of its formality, but in dribs and drabs, strung out through the better part of a morning, in old cars and big modern trucks and aluminum Airstream house trailers. These they'd crowd into one corner of the lot and they served them for sleeping, eating, and office facilities for the next few weeks. There were roustabouts and ferris wheel proprietors and merry-go-round operators and high-wire trapeze artists, fortune-telling gypsies, and pitchmen who operated the wheels of chance. Male and female, these were the people who, in two days flat, could turn a vacant lot into a veritable Babylon of exotic adventure and entertainment.

It was excitement of the first order. They surrounded our own little wooden shacks with gaudily painted structures, a glassed-in candy-apple booth, a giant bingo tent, a two-rank merry-go-round with mirrors and a calliope which shrieked out strange, unfamiliar European waltzes and gallops, and a ferris wheel which fielded twelve cars and topped out well over the roof of my house across the street. Over everything were strung crossed lines of electric lights which provided more dazzling candlepower than Princess Anne had ever concentrated in one place.

The Monday of opening was a day of continuing fast-paced energy. By now the firemen volunteers and the carny people were hard at it, getting everything set for the first evening's operations. Prizes had to be brought in for bingo, soft drinks and dry ice lockers stocked, and the final kinks and glitches removed from the rudimentary public address system. Chief Raymond Carey, very important at his place on the bandstand, would blast forth a string of microphone tests, always ending with the one important question: "Can you all hear me over there?"

As evening approached, all would be in readiness. It was truly an impressive sight. Imagine standing at the intersection of Irving Avenue and Beechwood street, your back to the west and looking down toward the railroad tracks. The area from the south boundary of the new public library down to the old white frame Victorian home at the intersection of Beechwood and Washington is solid carnival.

Throughout the `thirties it was always laid out the same. I can still see it clearly. To your farthest right, at the far southeast reach of the area, stands the ferris wheel, its cars facing Beechwood Street. Just in front of the wheel, the carnival proprietors have leased a space to a high-wire act which features a white-spangled lady who makes a spectacular thirty-five foot dive into a drum of water no wider than six feet and which appears to have previously served as a cattle watering trough.

Fronting on the street at the south of the lot, Mrs. Ernestine Baltz has a while-you-wait photograph booth where for a quarter you could get three photographs which would last the night through before fading to a sickly brown. At the back of lot runs our row of little booths, each one rented by a local businessman and by now trimmed and painted and decked and brilliantly lighted until it looks quite respectable. Mr. Harold McAllen displayed the first front-loading gas-operated driers I ever saw. Eastern Shore Light and Power displayed new electric refrigerators alongside their Ready Kilowatt motif. C. H. Hayman and Sons Hardware had a display as did the Boy Scouts.

Facing up next to Irving Avenue at the front of the south lot was the bingo tent, erected by the carnival itself but run and operated by the firemen's ladies auxiliary. It was here that the greatest store of delightfully appalling prizes were displayed, a center pyramid flanked on all sides with lavender teddy bears and Betty Boop kewpie dolls and ladies with thermometers in their stomachs holding lighted lamps aloft. On all four sides, benches ran and on good nights you had to stand in line to get a seat and a five-cent Bingo card.

Across the street, the bandstand stood, bedecked in red, white, and blue star-spangled bunting. A large drum stood to one side of the steps where you could place your raffle tickets which were sold off every night ... good for a case of Pepsi and two pounds of country sausage from Elmer Newton's store, a lube and oil change from Bozman and Hall's Esso, that sort of thing. Tickets were drawn and their numbers read aloud on the public address system with great pomp and ceremony with the donor's name receiving appropriate emphasis.

In the far northeast corner in those earliest days stood the merry-go-round, the best noise-maker on the field, bar none, ablaze with lights like the stricken Titanic. Five cents was the cost of a single ticket. Moving from the merry-go-round back toward Irving Avenue you'd pass the gambling wheels (no pay-offs in money, only in more exotic toys and garish works of art). The ring-toss, always appearing so devilishly easy, giving you three rings for a nickel but minimal chances for success, was also located in this area. Next to the bandstand was the snowcone stand, pure shaved ice and flavored syrup in a paper cone and tasting amazingly good on a hot night.

When viewed from your vantage point on the sidewalk across Beechwood Street, the whole thing awash with light, blasting with overlapping recorded music from two or three separate sources, the amplified voices of the barkers, and jammed with people at shoulder-to-shoulder distances, it was an impressive spectacle. Even week nights brought good crowds.

It would start out quietly enough, around seven o'clock. The firemen would be at their stations, manning the wheels of chance, the soft drink counters and the hot dog stand. The `27 American LaFrance fire--engine, chrome and paint a-gleam, would be parked somewhere in evidence, the newest thing we had. The old `23 Ford would be back in the fire-house in case of fire. I was always on hand at the this grand opening, along with a half-dozen others who lived close by. Presently, toward dark the crowd would pick up and I'd see classmates from school, friends from Perryhawkin and King's Creek and Oriole whom I'd not seen since school let out in May, and soon we'd be running and chasing each other for old times sake and being totally and enthusiastically boisterous and noisy.

For some reason we never rode the rides until after it was good and dark and the light bugs swarmed in torrents around the lights and pelted you hard like BB's. The merry-go-round was more spectacular in the dark and the ferris wheel was the most delight of all as you'd rock dangerously back and forth in the free-hanging seat (it can't flip over, everybody assured you) and look down at the grounds and the surrounding darkness, back to the swamp at the foot of Irving Avenue and up to the whole of main street in front of you. It was fun, even at eight and nine, for me and a friend to get one poor unsuspecting girl between us on the three-place seat. Rocking as hard as we could, she'd add to the merriment by screaming appropriately loud. And as you came down, we'd all cheer as the operator throttled up the old engine in one more loud exhaust blast and lift us high again into the dark night for at least one more turn.

Toward nine or nine-thirty, Mother wanted me in the house to get ready for bed so after one more snowcone, I'd take my leave. And with the carnival just across the street and the windows wide open for what ever breeze there might be, I'd lie in bed, sweaty and hot and listen to the recorded music of Lulu Belle and Skyland Scotty and the insistent amplified Bingo-drone of B-8, N-32, O-64.

Towards eleven, or whenever the crowd appeared to be thinning, they'd draw for the evening's raffles and everybody cheered the winners. As the last final attraction, the high-wire artists would make their appearance, guaranteeing that nobody would go home until they began their act, thereby allowing the firemen to milk the last nickel out of those determined to stick it out.

Then the ferris wheel would bark to a stop and the lights would dim and soon the place was as quiet as a cemetery A quiet breeze would spring up from the east and in moments I'd be sound asleep.

*   *   *

The next morning began early. The nighttime carnival was for everybody but those of us who lived on Beechwood street were allowed to be a part of what went on during the day. To go to the carnival grounds during the day was to be an insider.

Ralph Dryden, Milbourne Witt, the two grandchildren of Mr. Sam Richardson, Craig and Suzanne Metz, and Hazelbelle, Carolyn, and Lola Jean Hampton, the three little-girl nieces of Mr. Walter Mc-Dowell, and perhaps Jimmy Austin and I would roam the hot, dry grounds, kicking sawdust, talking to the carnival workers, unsuccessfully trying to stay out of the way, and soaking up the unique culture of these strange itinerant people.

The men all had the same three-day growth of whiskers, never clean shaven, never bearded. They were red-eyed, sweaty, and none too clean and carried their cigarettes rolled into the sleeves of their stained Tee-shirts. The fire-eater at one sideshow showed us how to swallow fire without burning ourselves but none of us tried. We'd beg for free rides on the ferris wheel while the wheel captain did his routine maintenance. I had a special "in" with these fellows; they'd go over to the faucet in our side yard for buckets of drinking water. This was enough to gain me an extra two or three rotations on the merry-go-round every evening.

We'd climb on the cab of the huge eighteen-wheeler Diamond-T equipment truck and look in awe at the gypsy fortune teller lady with her sleek black hair and dangling cigarette and wonder why she wore so much jewelry and so little of anything else. In the heat of the afternoon, we'd crawl under the bandstand to stay cool and tell each other stories while above somebody worked with the sound system, playing *God Bless America* over and over again.

Sometime during the last week, there'd be the great Firemen's Parade. It would start on South Main Street, work its way up to Broad Street and then proceed to the carnival grounds. Volunteers from as far away as Chestertown would come to Princess Anne, with fire engines, a few dozen men in ranks, and if they were lucky, a firemen's band of another two dozen or so. It was the greatest of the town's annual spectacles. Main Street would be packed and everybody would come around to the grounds, tagging along behind the last element of the parade.

This was a wonderful time for Chief Raymond Carey and Mr. Marion Austin, Mr. Clarence Phillips and other staunch members of the fire department to get up on the bandstand, sharp in their dark-blue and nickel-trimmed uniforms, and welcome other companies and get their pictures taken. Then each band would take a turn on the bandstand and pump out their own versions of *Our Director March* and such others as they could manage. People packed the grounds elbow to elbow on Parade Night.

Toward the end of the second week, the excitement would build up as we'd speculate about the big raffle. In 1940, the fire company raffled off a new cream-colored Mercury two-door and we'd all tell each other what we'd do if we won it. The Mercury had been paraded around the streets of Princess Anne for a good two months, a big sign on its roof offering chances for a dollar. It would be, by the last night of the carnival, considerably less than spanking new.

We'd all stay late for the drawing was always the last thing of the last night. Someone spun the drum and as I remember, amid blaring music and considerable hoopla, the car went to Roy Alder who drove it for the many years of the war which followed.

I don't remember much about the days immediately following. One just didn't hang around to watch the desecration of anything so won- derful as the Princess Anne Firemens' Carnival. The carny workers struck their equipment late during the last night and by dawn would be on their way up the shore to Smyrna or Denton or wherever they were next booked.

The War saw the end of the firemen's carnival and when peace came again, Mr. Claude Wiles had built a beautiful frame bungalow just where the merry-go-round should have stood and his garage occupied the ring-toss. It was down-hill from then on. Later it moved itself over to the auction block grounds, and still later on, I guess, the American Legion took on the carnival-holding job for the town.

But it wasn't as good as it used to be. But then things never are.

Going to the Movies in Princess Anne

In my grandparents' time, the youngest of children learned of the world and its wonders through story telling. Later, when they were older, they had books, great leather-bound things with fine type and steel engravings of pyramids and kings and the Summer Palace of the Tsar and such. My children had television, neatly packaged programs like *Bold Journey* and an occasional *National Geographic* special. I fell somewhere in between. I had movies. I had the Preston, Princess, and Auditorium theaters. So did everybody else.

It was a common culture and it was good. It guaranteed, if nothing else that we'd all play the same pretend-game for an entire week. *Drums Along the Mohawk* put all of us in an Indian-fighting mood. *Dawn Patrol* made us all into instant World War One aviators. None of this 'What-channel-did-you-watch-last-night?' business. We all saw precisely the same thing at the same time. It was generally on Saturday and almost always at one of Mr. Earl Morris's movie theaters.

In the heyday of the Silver Screen, Princess Anne had two movie houses, the short-lived Auditorium on the second floor of the old brick building south of the bank on Main Street which housed the post office, and the big, glorious theater across from the Washington Hotel. That theater, over my own lifetime, had borne three separate names, the *Preston,* the *Princess,* and the *Arcade.* There may have even been other names earlier, back in the 'twenties, but I wasn't around then to take note.

My first recollection of the movies was so early in my life that it's all muddled with other very-young memories ... a big, dark, stark, barny place called the Preston where Mother would take me on Saturday afternoons to the matinee. At two or three years old, it wasn't for my benefit so much as hers. She'd scrub me up properly and dress me in very clean clothes and off we'd walk uptown to the movies. Sitting by her side I remember my first visions of a light-house with grizzled men in Sou'Westers and a raging storm along a gray rock-strewn coast. I remember a strange movie showing the bazaars of Egypt, all done in green and white tints and I remember seeing what was perhaps the first commercial film in "color", a movie with Eddie Cantor in which only the last reel was printed in a strange purple and blue and red hue.

I remember too, when Lucretia, our maid, told me about a wonderful comedy she'd seen. It was, she said, called *Our Gang*, and it was all about funny little boys and girls and dogs having really good times together. She made it sound so good that I couldn't wait until my Saturday matinee and so I made Lucretia tell me the story over and over again until she was tired of it.

There was a fire sometime back in 1935 or '36 and the Preston was severely damaged. When it reopened sometime later, it was no longer the Preston, but the Princess. What we did for entertainment in the interim I don't remember. It must have been unsettling. Back then, everybody spent a lot of time at the movies.

The Princess was totally and thoroughly grand, the grandest thing I'd ever seen. Gone were the gray walls and stark, utilitarian overhead light fixtures and harsh seats. Mr. Morris had tried to afford the town with an absolutely elegant theater in the opulent style that was so popular everywhere, but still done in keeping with a typical Princess Anne set of values so that nobody could complain that it was over-fancy.

There was a red velour of sorts along both side walls, with little lights set into recesses and there were carpets along the two aisles. But the ceiling was wonderful too and I remember resting my head on the back of the seat and looking up at that ceiling with its parallel rows of undulating soft blue and silver stripes, like ribbons of satin all running lengthwise of the theater. The curtain was a heavy red velvet and there was a little stage forward where people could put on talent shows and Vaudeville acts if the occasion arose.

It was under these blue and silver ribbons that many of my future values and value-judgements must have been formed. The virtues of a pure heart and curly hair and love and loyalty to family and friends were brought home to me time and time again by Shirley Temple in each of the dozens of her movies I sat through. (Shirley also helped to germinate my earliest seeds of cynicism: It was all made-up. Nobody in real life could ever be that darned sweet!) Background music played constantly. I was almost grown before I could see a pretty girl and not hear the subtle sweeping violins of an Erik Corngold soundtrack somewhere in the background. I still do, on occasions.

An early-on rite of passage occurred when you were old enough to go to the movies by yourself. This generally happened at about six. Initially the privilege was extended only to Saturday afternoon matinees with the understanding that you'd come right home after the movie. Your parents had to have faith in you but more importantly, Miss Annie Morris Rufenacht had to have faith in you. Mr. Earl Morris might have owned the Princess lock, stock, and barrel, but Miss Annie was its ticket-seller and its Governor-General, make no mistake about it.

Miss Annie was stern and faithful to her duties and, to my recollection, never took a vacation. She was there in the glassed-in ticket booth which sat in the middle of the front corridor from my earliest remembrances until, I suppose, the theater just sort of died. She functioned with businesslike efficiency, taking dimes and nickels, scarcely ever smiling overly much. She eyed each of us with a certain look of skepticism. "I know your kind," it seemed to say. "You're not here to see *The Desert Song* with Dennis Morgan and I know it. You're only here to run up and down the aisle like a bunch of wild Indians and whoop and holler and in general misbehave and if you even so much as think about it, you're all out of here quicker than scat." We became skilled at translating her thoughts.

There was another rite of passage six or so years later. The day you became twelve, Miss Annie charged you full admission, fifteen cents instead of ten or twelve which was the going rate for children. This presented everybody with a problem, not excluding Miss Annie. Your natural inborn respect for money made you want to continue on at the old rate until you were at least twenty-one. On the other hand, twelve years old was not an inconsiderable milestone, one that marked a watershed in the process of growing up.

Our decisions usually fell on the side of good concrete dollars and cents rather than on any abstract watershed and so we'd walk short and try to sneak through. Miss Annie, I firmly believe, had a friend in the

Board of Education who regularly sent her the names of everybody in school recently turned twelve. She'd eye you even more firmly than usual and then look down silently and disapprovingly at the dime and two miserable pennies you'd given her and finally shame you into digging down for the extra three cents.

The Princess was divided into three or four principal areas. Mr. Morris didn't plan most of it that way. It just sort of worked itself out. Down-front were three rows of old solid wood seats, probably from before the fire. Here and only here was any amount of cutting-up even tolerated. If you were five or six or seven and your mother would let you, you'd sit down-front where you could wiggle and squirm and stand up if it pleased you, swipe somebody's hat for pass-along, and maybe bop somebody else on the head with a balloon. You could eat Tootsie--Rolls and chunk the wrappings at a friend. Anything went so long as you were quiet about it.

Starting at about the fifth row back, it grew more and more respectable, and well-behaved fourth- and fifth-graders who were totally civilized would sit there. By mid-theater it was civil enough for ladies and gentlemen and babies. Good solid citizens always sat middle-center. The forward side seats to the right of the two aisles were hardly ever used unless the movie was a real sell-out. Only strange people would sit there otherwise. Back row of center was, by consent, reserved for those on call, the patrolman who stopped in for a minute to get warm, doctors, nurses, and the like. It was too far back and set too deeply under the balcony to be prime seating.

The back rows over on the left tier of seats facing the screen were for those in their teens. Nobody under high-school age would dare to sit there. It's where you would sit if you had a date. The further toward the back and the left you got, the more heady became the atmosphere until you reached that ultimate pinnacle of teen-age abandonment, the last two corner seats. To take a girl back there was the equivalent of announcing your engagement.

These were coveted seats during the war when gas rationing cut dramatically into the number of slow nighttime drives you could make out to Allen by way of Pine Pole Road. Soldiers and their dates bought movie tickets like there was no tomorrow and threatened, by sheer weight of numbers, to spill over into those areas of the theater where they shouldn't have been.

When the lights came up after the Coming Attractions, there was always a great amount of shuffling and straightening and smoothing and setting things aright and when I was still eleven, I'd cast quick little sideways glances to see who had the most to straighten. Somehow, to me, it seemed that tacit permission to sit left-side rear would be yet another rite-of-passage I'd yet have to take. It came much easier than that.

One evening in late forty-four as a Freshman in high school, I walked in immediately behind a charming girl who, although still in the seventh grade, was one of my very favorite people. Danny Kaye was playing in *Up in Arms* and without thinking too much at all about it, we both sat down together in that singularly dedicated section, the infamous left-side rear. I could, by virtue of being thirteen and in high school, she also because she was sitting with me.

Nothing happened. Nothing at all. Had it been a grade B-George Raft gangster movie, who's to say what kind of dreadful carryings-on there might have been that night? But it was Danny Kaye with his mugging and great scat-singing and at the end we were both red-faced and exhausted from laughing.

Then there was the balcony. That was the one area Mr. Morris had planned as a separate and distinct area from the start. It was, in the vernacular of the time, the "Colored Balcony." The Balcony extended over the wings of the lower seats and was supported by pillars. It was divided into two halves, roughly, with the projection booth separating them. We all bought our tickets together, with balcony admission a few cents cheaper than ours, but that's as far as it went. When we pushed through the twin metal doors, we were separate and, hopefully, equal. Two staircases flanked the arcade at the inside of the doors and they'd peel off from the crowd, climbing the stairs to the balcony for what, objectively, was the better view of the screen.

The Princess was a good theater with Mr. Morris supplying good value for the dollar. He worked hard at it and was there almost every night, strolling up and down the aisles in that heavy, leisurely, contemplative gait of his, keeping an eye on every living thing within. You'd see him move to the front rows, silhouetted against the screen, and then, at a quiet part in the movie, you'd hear his gruff voice: "You stop that or I'm gonna make you leave, y'hear?" And then back up the aisle, keeping a wary eye on left-side rear. "Hey, you know better'n that. Put that cigarette out."

The year 1939 marked the peak year for Hollywood, quantity-wise if not quality. They turned out films by the hundreds at a rate not exceeded either before or since. Movies were big business and the Princess was full every night Monday through Thursday, jammed on Friday and jam-packed on Saturday night when all of the farm people came to town and sent the youngsters to the movies while they shopped. With overflow crowds, Mr. Morris re-opened the Auditorium.

The Auditorium was once a real auditorium in the true sense of the word. It was a popular place for dances and cotillions and Chatauquas and the like, but that was before my time. So far as I knew, it was vacant until perhaps early 1940 when it was re-opened as a Friday- and Saturday-night-only overflow movie theater.

Going to the Auditorium was an unnerving experience for one raised on the gentilities of the Princess. At best, it was a functional, no-frills theater. Mr. Morris had no illusions. He gave you considerably less and so charged less too, by a nickel or so and you always got a double feature and a serial. You went up a flight of stairs flanking the entrance to the Post Office, made a sharp left at the top of the stairs, and walked down a short corridor. There at the end was Miss Alice Morris behind a glass window, smiling and ready to take your dime.

You'd then push your way through two black canvas swinging doors and look for a vacant seat beside a friend. The dark and gloom of the old Preston had been miraculously resurrected in the Auditorium. Two colors predominated, brown and gray, a third if you'll accept black. The floor was dark, greasy hardwood. The screen was unadorned by a curtain and the projector was in all likelihood itself a fugitive from the Preston. The whole place smelled like beer but it was probably only the aroma of the Gunthers filtering up from Henry Morris's restaurant next door down below.

But it was fun, fun in a way that the Princess never was. For one thing, nothing ever worked quite right and that was the charm of the place. You could prop your feet up on the back of the chair in front of you if it was empty and nobody even cared. Smoking, always forbidden at the Princess and any other civilized theater, was not only permitted but seemed like a social obligation. Half way through the first feature the air would be so thick and blue with cigarette and cigar smoke that today's Environmental Protection Agency people would likely have padlocked the doors forever. The high point of any performance was the scheduled breakdown of the projector and the sudden darkening of the theater. This allowed everybody to holler and scream and clap hands and stomp feet loudly and kiss a girl so as to hurry the projectionist along with his repairs.

The best thing about the Auditorium were the movies themselves. Movies so old and terrible that they'd never make it anywhere else were the usual fare and were good grounds for a noisy, running scene-by-scene critique from all of the sixth and seventh graders in the audience. A Western so simple-minded as to make Hopalong Cassidy appear almost urbane was always good for starters. We pointed out each defect loudly and with enthusiasm and laughter. The last feature of the evening was scarcely ever as good as grade B although I do remember some great old Dick Powell and Myrna Loy films from the early thirties, put out to pasture after their sprocket holes had succumbed to fatigue.

The Serial, always a standard sixteen-chapter affair, fell between the cowboy and the Grade-B. The Serial provided us with more delights than any of the features because we could always boo and hoot at the marvelously contrived disasters to which the bad guys subjected the male lead and from which he always escaped at the beginning of the next episode.

None of my friends in the sixth grade ever took the Serial seriously. But there was one person in the audience who *did* take it all to heart, an actual adult, one poor grown-up man. That serial was the highlight of his week. He lived through the hum-drum of his stock room job at the grocery store in a state of considerable agitation just waiting for the next Friday night and then it would start up all over again. I can see him now, looking around to where we were sitting and he'd peer at us through his thick glasses and tell us boys not to worry ourselves because the hero, chances are, wasn't even in the factory when it blew up anyhow.

There was never a short subject or a cartoon or any Coming Attraction previews. Mr. Morris never bothered with Coming Attractions. At the Auditorium you took what movies he offered. It was theater-in-the-rough.

Having two theaters in town was a luxury. Friday nights I'd head for the Auditorium while Saturday evenings were reserved for the more sedate fare of the Princess. The Princess was the sort of quality place where you could put on your best sport coat and Argyll socks and feel right about taking any girl. And Carey's soda fountain right next door was available if you had an extra nickel or two and a really serious need to impress her. The Princess represented our 1940's idea of real class. The Auditorium didn't.

Sometime in the late `forties or early `fifties, long after I had more important things to do than go to the movies, the Arcade theater on Salisbury's West Main Street burned. All that was left was the magnificent metal-and-glass Art Deco marquee. Somewhere around this time, the old wooden portico which stretched over the sidewalk in front of the Princess became tired and worn. It was a natural conjunction for Mr. Morris and one day a truck brought the huge marquee down from Salisbury and down came the portico which I'd known all of my life. This new thing was a spectacular structure, with the name ARCADE still standing high and proud in big block letters. It seemed to be just the touch to spruce up the old Princess.

Mr. Morris wasn't one to spend a lot of money when other equally good options were available to him at lower cost. It could have been costly to unbolt the six ARCADE letters and replace them with all-new letters which said PRINCESS. Why not, he must have reasoned, just change the name of the place? It'd be a lot cheaper. And so the Princess went the way of all things and the Arcade came about.

It wasn't the same. For months I continued to call it the Princess but later on I took the easy route out and found myself referring to the Arcade. But I knew it wasn't and it shouldn't have been. One can become reactionary and crotchety, even in his `teens.

I remember no movies worth remembering from the Auditorium. It was more of a place to experience than to see a movie. All of my great movie memories come from the Princess. It was there I saw *Pinocchio* and *Snow White* and was thoroughly enchanted. It was there I missed *The Wizard of Oz* because I had been over-fed on Shirley Temple movies and at ten I was in no mood for any more cute little girls who sang, even if they came from Kansas.

It was there I saw *Casablanca* for the first of many viewings. I learned the basics of flying an airplane at six from watching a series of Frank Hawks shorts in which he gave the audience flying lessons which were so thorough that they stood me in advantage the first time I ever flew. I sat through every Abbot and Costello film ever made. I saw *Dodge City* and *Citizen Kane* and *Gone with the Wind*. I was so thoroughly conditioned by Hollywood that I even made up and hummed my own little bits of proper background music at appropriate and crucial times.

I was entertained but I was also instructed in the morals and principles of society as only the movies could do it. I learned a certain brand of patriotism from countless war movies. From Warner Brothers and their scores of prison movies I learned that if I did bad things, the cops would come and get me and put me in jail forever. I believed it as firmly as I could believe anything. I still do.

Shirley Richards tells me that the theater is still there, locked up like a time capsule. Sometime when I'm down that way, I'd like to go in and have a look and stand for a minute among the ghosts and shades of old black-and-white morality. I'd like to sit down and prop my head back on the seat and stare upwards and see that undulating blue and silver ribboned ceiling again. It covers a lot of memories.

Elementary to High School - Crossing the Great Divide

W hen I pick up a local paper and read about the public schools in Montgomery County, Maryland's wealthiest county, I get a disconcerting feeling that our current school system belongs to another world. It's a strange and foreign world made up of middle schools, junior highs, and special-interest schools, and magnet schools, pre-kindergartens, restructured vocational training schools and other sorts of strangely named and expensive institutions which I couldn't have attended, even if I'd known what they were all about.

When I grew up in the 1930's in Princess Anne we went to Princess Anne Elementary School for seven years and then to Washington High School for another four. Then you were on your own. No Junior High, no specialized schools where you could take strange courses to prepare you to be something that your father wasn't and your family wouldn't have approved of anyway. That was it. Elementary School and then High School. And all in eleven years. It was the way that things had always been done. I did remember that my Grandfather would talk about "grade school" but I knew in my heart that he really meant "elementary school".

It was a narrow, high-sided educational channel through which we passed and we weren't allowed much compass deviation in any direction. If you were from town, it would all start on some bright September morning when you were shooed into the first grade at Princess Anne Elementary School. We entered through the big double glassed doors which led directly into a large, central auditorium. Immediately to our left was the first grade room, the first point on a big circle of rooms surrounding the auditorium. From there, you proceeded apace, year by year, second grade, third grade, and so on, in a clockwise direction until seven years later you ran out of rooms and had no place to go other than out.

Out meant high school. The Board of Education never seemed to concern itself overly much about the abruptness of this transition. On their long road to maturity our children are fed ever bigger bites of education in smooth, painless, and mitered doses. It flows like tooth-paste, pre-packaged from pre-kindergarten to post-graduate school and heavens-knows where else. But when we viewed the smug, cozy little clubhouse of our seventh grade class in 1944, the transition from ele-mentary school to high school seemed as abrupt and as shaking as a train wreck, a right of passage in growing up which was second only to being drafted and sent to the Pacific Theater to fight the Japs.

Elementary school was structured like your family. Your classmates were like your brothers and sisters. You lived with them and poked them across the aisle and giggled, and ate with them and fought with them at recess. Your teacher was Mother, Grandmother all in one. She was God in a flowered cotton smock. In the next room around that great circle, you had bigger brothers and sisters. Away up in the seventh grade, you had some very big brothers and sisters who never bothered to talk to you very often. Your life was centered nine months out of the year in this ornate brick building with the white Doric columns called Princess Anne Elementary School.

Across town was Washington High School. It seemed a formidable place. During our early years we viewed it from afar. Like marriage and other grown-up things, we all knew that some day we'd be faced with going to high school, but that was far, far away and there were too many other things to think about. Besides, we knew we were all too little to understand it so there was no reason to worry about it.

Words like "intermural" and "sophomore" and "junior prom" came to my mind whenever I thought about high school. I wasn't even sure what they all meant. Not having an older brother or sister in high school required that I learn everything I knew on the subject from Judy Garland and Mickey Rooney movies. High schools were about dates and varsity letters and football games and homecoming queens and really tough final exams. The only thing I really knew first-hand about high school was that high-schoolers were as big as grown-ups and carried their books in book-straps while we in Princess Anne Ele-mentary always used book bags. They also never talked to people in elementary school. In this last matter, they were worse than seventh-graders.

But we, like the hand of a giant, slowly moving clock, gradually made our clockwise way through the classrooms surrounding the big auditorium, and with each passing year high school became a more urgent and pressing reality. No longer was it some vague distant island on a misty horizon. It was now looming larger by the month, with strange and perplexing and somewhat frightening topography all coming more sharply into view as we prepared for our landfall. One real promontory was "Home Room".

* * *

I first heard the term "home room" one spring afternoon. Jane Richards told me about it. Jane lived next door, was a good two years older than I, and was my final authority on everything having to do with Washington High School. It was she who first warned me about the terrible things the high school seniors would do to me if they ever caught me sitting on the near-sacred ceremonial outdoor brick bench with the lintel of the old Washington Acadamy mortared into its back. But there was something sort of disquieting and disturbing about the off-hand and easy way she dropped the word home room into our conversation. My schoolroom was my home room. I lived there with Jack and Francis and George and Joyce and Reba and Tommy Evans and everybody else. Nobody ever called it our "home" room anymore than they called the cafeteria the "eating" cafeteria. Some things were self-evident.

"What do you mean, home room?" I asked, stressing the *home* part. I tried to sound casual. But torn between my natural inclination to want to appear worldly and knowledgeable and my desire to find out about this briar patch into which I'd soon be tossed, I chose the latter.

"It's where you go first thing in the morning," she said. "For opening exercises and announcements. And you leave your coat there."

"Then what?"

"You change classes. You might go to English or maybe math."

But we all go off somewhere together, right?," I said, hoping to make it sound like I was confronting an established fact. In the seventh grade we changed classes every afternoon, all of us picking up our books and trooping next door to Miss May Cannon's room for geography class.

"Uh-uh. You just might not have classes with anybody in your home room. And you have your own personal class schedule that you'll have to memorize. They'll give it to you the first day."

I could imagine it ... off on my own in those vast halls of Washington High School, guided only by my personal class schedule and surrounded by total strangers, looking in vain for a familiar face. My mind leaped ahead to a time a few years in the future when I'd see Ted Phoebus on the street in front of the Hotel and we'd stare hard at each other's faces, each trying to recollect who the other one was. "Oh," he'd say. "You're Frank Pierce. We went to elementary school together, didn't we?"

I tried to make the best of it. "Well at least, everybody in my English class will be an eighth-grader."

"No. Might be from any class. You could have a Junior in your math class if he's flunked algebra twice."

I didn't like the word "flunked" either. "Failed" was what we'd always called it. And you failed a grade. You didn't flunk a course. "You mean a tenth-grader in my eighth-grade arithmetic class?" I asked.

"Junior in your Freshman class." She corrected me with a casual kind of knowing sophistication and just the slightest bit of condescension. ..."in your *math* class. What course are you going to take?"

I was stumped. "All of them?" It wasn't an answer so much as an unsuccessfully phrased question.

"No. Don't be silly. I mean are you going to take the Academic course, Commercial, General course, the Agriculture program with the FFA?"

I shook my head. I hadn't given it much thought.

"You've got pretty good marks so they'll probably put you in the academic course. They always do, if you have good marks." That was good, I thought. At least it was one decision I didn't have to make for myself.

"Of course," she added, deliberately thinking out loud to herself for my benefit, "The Academic course ... that's the hard one. You have to take trigonometry and Latin and physics and if you flunk just one course you might have to stay a Freshman for another year. And lots of people flunk." Jane's attitude was worldly, that of one wanly resigned to the injustice of it all. Her outlook on life gloried in the worst-case scenario.

She then went on to explain about things like study hall. "They might assign you to a Senior class study hall," she'd tell me, by now totally enjoying my discomfort. "They'll sit you in the back of some class with a teacher you don't even know, probably. For an hour every day," she added for good measure.

My world was fragmenting. Sophomores would be bad enough. Seniors would kill me, probably. The friendly, clubby little group of kids who'd been together since heavens-knows-when and who were now at the pinnacle of our elementary school existence was about to be shattered and scattered but there was no getting around it. Graduation was inevitable. Come September and I'd be in high school, like it or not.

Spring turned to early June and graduation. Somebody from the *Marylander and Herald* took our class picture, boys in blue jackets and white pants and girls in white summer dresses, in front of the big white columns. Amidst the perfume of lilacs and flags, Principal Bill Evans slowly paraded our class to the stage with the stately strains of *War March of the Priests* which he majestically drummed out on the piano with proper pomp and ceremony. Superintendent of Somerset County Schools C. Allen Carlson spoke to us, the class of 1944, Princess Anne Elementary School, in final assembly and I would have been happy if he'd given us a reprieve and told us we could stay on another year because we were all needed right there where we were to help the war effort.

But he didn't. Off we went. And thinking back, it wasn't too bad, not even the first day. Principal C. N. Baughan gathered us in the auditorium, chuckled softly over his own jokes and talked to us and sounded almost like any other teacher and didn't use any of the sorts of words I couldn't understand.

It was all there, just as Jane had described it. There were home rooms and the academic curriculum and math and French. First period in the afternoon, off I went to study hall and found myself sitting all by myself at the rear of the room where they taught Senior-year French, staring at the backs and necks of some very adult-looking young ladies. But somehow it didn't seem at all frightening.

It took a little bit of getting used-to. And it wasn't bad. At least it wasn't nearly as bad as I'd figured it to be. I didn't get lost in the halls, not even once and somehow, it just blended itself into a kind of pleasant seamless continuity which continued on until one day in my senior year when they sat us down to take our college-level entrance board examinations. I was scared. But then, I'd been scared before.

Row-Boating on the Manokin

A good county map will mark the Manokin River as something of consequence, its headwaters up in the upper part of the county, mouth on Tangier Sound, a river so broad that you can't see across to Rumbley and Fairmount if you try to sight them from Wenona. But if you stand on the town bridge today and look first upstream and then down, the Manokin looks like somebody tried to civilize it; there's a distinct drainage-ditch quality about it.

It was not always so. Not when I was a boy back in the 1940's. Those straight banks and angular bends have come about as a consequence of many attempts at flood control which consumed considerable State and Federal engineering time over the past few decades. The River is now reasonably well behaved and properly mannered, scarcely ever flooding its banks. As a river, it is also considerably more boring.

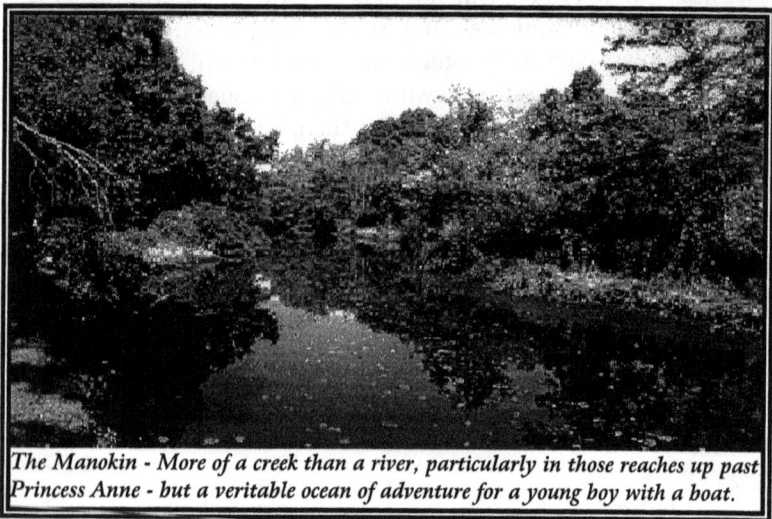

The Manokin - More of a creek than a river, particularly in those reaches up past Princess Anne - but a veritable ocean of adventure for a young boy with a boat.

But in the 1940's everything was comparatively natural. Rivers came to you pretty much in the condition that God had made them and people accepted the fact that, upon occasions, they would flood their bank and wash away houses. That's just the way things are, they said. No reason to complain too much for it won't do any good anyway.

I knew that river as well as anybody. But we didn't call it a river. It was a creek. I spent a good portion of my youngest days living in the big green house which borders it just north of the bridge and I grew up rowing a flat-bottomed skiff a mile or so up from the bridge down to Red Bridge over the Deal Island Road and a little beyond. My earliest memory is of the big hurricane in 1933, the one which cut the inlet between the ocean and Sinepuxant Bay at Ocean City, and how the storm caused the Manokin to burst its banks and flood our house. Our house, it seems, flooded with disconcerting regularity.

It was a snaking, meandering tidal river then, existing in its natural state, forever changing and modifying its banks as it wound its way down from up-County. Its banks were lined with willow trees, marsh grass, swamp cabbages, and cat-nine tails. Hummocks and protrusions formed and eroded away, to be replaced by more of the same after the spring floodings of the next year. Little child-sized islands were created where a snag would catch dirt and debris as it swept down stream and the island would last for two, maybe three years, long enough to grow a crop of silky green grass, long enough for me to give it a name and draw maps of it and claim it for my own.

My grandfather, who was born in 1858, swore that he could remember when sailing ships docked at the bridge with a fathom of safe water under their keels, but I suspect that he may have heard that story so often that he'd come to believe it himself. But legend does tell us that once the river stretched from the old Custom House on Broad Street on its south bank to the cemetery of the Presbyterian churchyard on its north with all else between being under water. And indeed, Princess Anne itself owes its existence to the Manokin. Situated right up where the headwaters were narrow enough to be called "the wading place", it was natural that, back in 1733, the Shore's earliest settlers would found a town there.

But by 1940 the Manokin had reduced its pretensions considerably, silted up from two centuries of up-county farming. North of the town bridge, it had no channel worth the name. The silt and run-off had so filled it in that to drown yourself in it would have taken a conscious, destructive effort. Up there, north of town it was barely six feet across with a quarter of a mile of marsh grass on the flood plain on either bank. On down-stream from the town bridge was only a little bit better. There you could get a rowboat through even at low tide.

But it was tidal and that's what made the Manokin fascinating to me. The water ran both ways, twice a day. The tides held promise of a perpetual change. When I was nine or ten, it was great excitement to stuff an old mayonnaise jar with a note, walk down in the back yard to the river bank and heave it in, firm in the knowledge that it would go to England or Madagascar or some such place on the next outgoing tide. High tide filled the river to the top of the banks and on a spring evening, it was quite pretty, almost pastoral. A flood tide would cover the marshes on the east side of the river to a depth of several inches and a heron would stand stately one-legged in the blue twilight and you could almost believe it was the Great Missouri River or some such place. It was a lot prettier than it was on low tide with the discarded oil drums from the old Maryland State Road garage exposed on the black-bottom mud.

In the spring of 1943, I was given a beautiful little flat-bottom rowboat, carefully and properly hand-constructed by a retired waterman named Windsor who lived in Somerset Heights and built it in his back yard. Stem to stern it was twelve feet long and could comfortably hold three boys, uncomfortably four, if two sat in the stern. Of all of the presents I ever got, nothing ever equaled that boat. It broadened my whole base of adventuring. We christened it *The Ensign*.

Having my own boat gave me a natural extension to the range of my Saturday morning wanderings into places which were totally isolated and unscarred by civilization. Adults, because they were blessed with better sense than we, never willingly ventured on the Manokin river. They had no contact with it, save as a swamp, a natural boundary to the back of their property, a place to lose an occasional cow to quicksand.

And having a boat gave me as the boat owner an absolute guarantee of lots of company on Saturdays, just as many of us have since discovered now that we've grown up and invested in our own boats and pay money every month to our local marina. By nine-thirty, there'd always be at least two others, ready to set sail with me. We had only a single decision to make on those Saturday mornings back in 1943. Do we go up-river from the town bridge or down?

It was largely a matter of the tide and when you'd guess it would change. A high tide just before cresting would give you the necessary water to get far upstream. And timing it properly would allow you to drift back down with the outgoing tide and still keep a few inches of water beneath your keel so that you didn't get stranded.

Going upstream was fundamentally a scary and chancy proposition. It wasn't an easy trip because, quite honestly, as you got out of sight of the town bridge, the river really wasn't much of a river. Rowing in our two-man style with a boy to each oar wasn't possible because even a rowboat takes a good six or seven feet of clearance on each side. But we'd row until we ran out of clear water and the banks closed in on us. Then we'd ship our oars inboard and pass one to the boy in the stern seat to pole us along. The river still a bit farther up would better be called a brook, with a sandy, pebble-strewed bottom with a good six or seven inches of water and this only on highest tide. To navigate, we'd all move to the stern to hold the bow as high as possible. It was a challenge, sort of like white-water rafting, except in slow motion.

South of the bridge on the river you're never out of sight of civilization but up north it was quiet and almost dismal, not a particularly happy place. If you had a foot of water under the keel, you'd be sure that, after a few more pushes by the fellow in the stern, that you'd be down to ten inches. Even the marsh got narrower and more constricted and the stands of scrub pine pressed themselves closer and closer to the banks. A half-hour upstream and you'd have the same feeling as though you were walking along a lonesome path through the woods. Even the birds were unnaturally quiet. The loudest sound would be the clunk of the oars in the oarlocks.

Although the map shows me that the river meanders in a north-eastward course up the county until it disappears somewhere around Eden, the practical extent, so far as we were concerned, was the railroad bridge which is situated about a half-mile due east of the point where old Route 13 joins the bypass north of town. A few hundred yards downstream from the railroad bridge, the riven bed swung sharply east and made its way through a series of little culvert-sized openings at the foot of the bridge. That final eastward swing formed the natural upper limits of our expedition. Beyond that was what the old explorers used to call Terre Incognito, the unknown and unexplored lands where no mariner dared to sail.

The railroad bridge was always there at our terminus, across that narrow corner of marsh, and the flood tide which had taken us so far from home was turning and the water beneath the keel was fast becoming an anemic little spigot-sized trickle. Turning the boat around was out of the question so we'd grab the remaining oar and turn to at the bow, polling stern-first downstream, the bow of the boat probably digging into the muddy creek bottom as one of us made his way up to the bow.

Going home with the tide was always best. Tides run more swiftly as they ebb and so we'd finally get ourselves turned around bow-foremost, sit at ease and watch the hummocks and ditch banks slip by while one of us sat in the stern, steering with the oar resting in the stern oarlock like a tiller. As we'd approach town the river would become alive again, with broad mudflats covered with marsh lilies and schools of brown minnows which never ventured up to where the creek narrowed.

A variant on this trip was to go up toward Bummyhook Bridge. The name is no longer used, I don't think, but Bummyhook was the little wooden bridge which crossed a little tributary of the Manokin just east of town on the way over to what was then called Princess Anne College. You can see it now but it's a concrete, culvertized Transportation Department-approved thing, and there's no way a boy could pole a rowboat beneath its footings.

I never think of that river-creek with those same mysterious longings except on certain days in Spring when the air is damp and moist and not yet warm and the first grasses catch hold in the footings of borders and bush-rows. And the sky is overcast and the snows and freezing times of the past winter are giving way to thousands of little liquid rivulets of fresh water. There's a smell to the air that I can't describe except it's one of pending and rudimentary life, and I can remember my grandfather, rising slowly, his body tired by eighty-plus years of work in and around that river. He'd pull on his gum boots and look out of the window at the sky and he too would sniff the air. "C'mon, Boy," he'd say to me, "High time to get that skiff in the water."

Aunt Liza and Other Anachronisms

The pattern doesn't fit with today's concepts of race and all of its problems. But then, very few things on the Eastern Shore of Maryland of the 1940's fitted in with today's ideas. They weren't necessarily opposite. They just didn't always agree.

If we read today's more socially conscious books and view the latest films, we see a great and unbridged chasm between those of us whom we quite naturally described as "white people" and those others whom we once called "colored people". Today, a generation of books and the output of hundreds of Black Studies programs have created a set of new stereotypes almost as vivid and idealized as the stereotypes of an earlier day, a smiling Aunt Jemima and a compliant, dutiful Uncle Ben. As usual, the Eastern Shore lay somewhere between the two, at least as I remember it.

And that's all I can say... or write about. Others may remember it differently. That's their right. And if they want to write about it, they've a perfect right to do so.

Two or three things stand out in my memory of that town. First, almost nobody in Somerset County had very much money, for it was the Great Depression. Few kept money in the bank for such cash as most people had was intended for immediate payment to somebody else come Saturday. And perhpas a handful of us, by chance, by position, or by luck of skin color, had a scant bit more than others. Second, we were about equally divided between black and white by population. Third, everyone was scrabbling too hard to survive to worry too much about his coloration. You were a farmer, or you worked the water down on the Bay, and you had bills to pay and children and the weather to worry about. You belonged to a church of some sort, and your neighbors expected a certain level of decency out of you. Somewhere, third or fourth down the list of important things, you were either white or colored. Color was no pressing problem at all and, where possible, was best ignored. But still, you always kept certain guiding rules in mind.

From the eyes of a little boy of three or four, the whole world of that time seemed to be populated by the dogs, the cats, and the people in the house and around the yard. I was taller than the cats and at least as tall as the dogs. The people were considerably taller than I, and I tried as best I could to stay out from underfoot. When you are, at best, three feet from the floor at eye level, race made no difference, even if you understood the concept, which I certainly didn't. Nobody ever told me that I was better than some and not as good as others. I knew only one thing. I was smaller. Further up the size-scale were parents, grandparents, aunts, uncles, and others, one of whom was Aunt Liza.

I moved for and obeyed Aunt Liza without question. I took it naturally. Everybody else in the house pretty much obeyed Aunt Liza Dennis. This wasn't strange because she was approaching the Century mark and had been in the kitchen forever. Although nobody ever made much over it when I was little, sitting over by the chimney in the big kitchen, I was in the presence of history.

It didn't seem strange either that Liza Dennis had been born a slave. By the time I was ten years old, I knew enough history to know as much or more about the institution of slavery as most other people in Princess Anne Elementary School. I knew slavery had been over and done for a long time. And to watch Aunt Liza, a small, wizened black woman, it was apparent, if nothing else, that she had been around for an equally long time. Her size was misleading. Although nature had given her a small, delicate frame, she added to it with creative clothing. She'd move through the kitchen in a rustle and flurry of petticoats and aprons, dresses, scarves, and kerchiefs and whatever else caught her fancy.

She began working for my grandfather decades before, apparently forever, because she had been a fixture in our kitchen when my own mother was born in 1905. Advancing years didn't confer on her any great gentling of her disposition or insights of wisdom that anyone might take notice of, but they did confer a certain sense of dignity and belonging and a sense of possessiveness about that kitchen. It was hers, make no mistake about it, former conditions of involuntary servitude notwithstanding.

Aunt Liza wasn't the standard elderly black, born into slavery during the waning days of the Civil War. Those were technical slaves at best, and they received lots of obituary space in the big-city newspapers when they died back in the 1960s purely because they were anachronistic curiosities. Those people, in all respect to them, knew nothing of slavery because they'd just been born to it and hadn't lived with it. Aunt Liza was the real thing. By best accounts, she was born sometime in the late 1830's but nobody was quite sure when. Her recollections stretched back far beyond the Civil War. She had been there and knew what it was all about.

By the time I was nine or ten, I'd come to hold her in a distant sense of wonder. But she scarcely took any notice of me, a small boy sitting in the chimney corner by the wood-box. She'd seen too many small boys sitting by too many wood-boxes to pay me any particular attention. She'd talk to my grandmother, the two of them discussing whatever the affairs of her day might be ... generally, I guess, what was for dinner and did she get the laundry clean enough.

And she'd talk to Lucretia. Aunt Liza, by the strength of her years, had graduated herself to the ranks of the supervisory. Lucretia was a little younger than my mother, and my grandmother had hired her on when she was scarcely in her teens, the plan being that Lucretia would work and Aunt Liza would supervise. This arrangement suited both parties. Lucretia was bright, full of energy, and anxious to learn. Aunt Liza was anxious to preserve her status as head of that kitchen. Teaching was only a secondary concern, as I remember it.

"I don't remember much about that old war," she told us. "Didn't fight any down here on the Eastern Shore, but I can remember one summer day when I was a good big girl, growd up, I `spect. Don't remember how old exactly. We was all out on the front lawn, and I was keeping an eye on the Dennis children and I heard all this booming and muttering coming from down in the southwest, out over the water. And it lasted all afternoon and into the next morning. Like thunder, just a-boomin' away. Nobody never told me what it was, but I guess it was the war."

I remember the story, every shred of it, even today. And common sense and a sense of history told me that Aunt Liza had heard the thunder of guns from Hampton Roads, down at Norfolk in 1862, when the Union Navy's *Monitor* took on the Confederate Navy's *Merrimack* in the Battle of the Ironclads. As the crow flies, it's well under a hundred miles, and sound carries well over those flat salt marshes which lay between Maryland's Somerset County and the mouth of the Chesapeake. Hardly anyone alive today has a recollection of a true story of the Civil War told by one who was there and a part of it. I did, and I'm glad.

Back then there was no social security for ancient and decrepit black women, no Medicaid to help them through their last illness. But they had something as good and almost as certain, an unwritten contract with those white people who'd hired them for next to nothing for a lifetime of productive work. And if you were to be a respectable white man or white woman in Princess Anne, as I remember it, you filled your end of the bargain. You continued on with those nickels and dimes and quarters under some face-saving pretense or another. You checked up on these old people, making sure there was wood in the wood box and food on the table. Fail to live up to your end of the bargain and people in town just might talk about you behind your back.

And so it was that, by1939 or 1940, Aunt Liza grew too feeble to carry on the pretense of cooking. The winter must have been hard, and at first she begged off coming over every day from her house on the other side of town. Spring came and by then the habit was ingrained. She never came back. But that wasn't to run up the white flag of surrender to advancing years, not a cause to give up everything she'd worked a lifetime for. By golly, Aunt Liza still had her place in the household and everyone had better recognize that fact. She announced, I was told, that she'd still take charge of the laundry, just as she had done for sixty or seventy years. No questions asked.

She told my grandmother, whom Aunt Liza probably considered to be not much older than the time in 1902 when my grandfather brought her home as a young bride of seventeen, "Miss Brown, you bring that laundry right here to me every Tuesday and every Friday. I don't trust nobody to do it right `sept me." My grandmother, whom I and almost everyone else regarded with considerable awe, apparently agreed. And every Tuesday I'd ride with her over to Aunt Liza's house, a bushel basket of dirty laundry in the trunk of the car. Friday it would be cleaned, starched, and folded perfectly. Cost? A quarter. Aunt Liza set a good price. It was what she'd been paid for a bushel of laundry for years.

My grandmother paid her thirty-five cents, as I remember. Thirty-five cents every week. She explained to me that Aunt Liza wasn't doing that washing and anybody with common sense knew that she wasn't. The quarter went to a great-grand-niece who lived next door. My grandmother paid the extra dime, she confessed, for "handling." The laundry contract that Aunt Liza negotiated at one-hundred years of age, continued on, unchallenged and unquestioned by anyone, until her death two years later. To do so would have been bad form, back in those days.

Taking care of people, as I was to find out, was more than simply providing money and checking the pantry. It sometimes involved difficult choices. Aunt Liza lived in a small frame house over in Greenwood with Charles, her son. Charles was an old man himself, a widower, probably into his seventies, none too cheerful as I recall, and given to a bit of hard drinking on occasions. But he was all she had in those last years of hers.

One time in the spring of 1941, Charles had had enough. On a Saturday night, the pressures of taking care of Aunt Liza got the better of him, and there'd been an awful row between Charles and his momma. Charles left the house in a rage, leaving the poor old woman alone and in tears. My grandmother caught wind of it through some inscrutable grape vine and on Sunday, she and I got in her car and drove out into the pine woods to the east of town to a small shack unfit for anything more particular than livestock or chickens as I recall. Inside was a rather chastened, and I assume now, hung-over Charles. She confronted him. "You get on home to your mother right now, she said sharply, "and tell her you're sorry." I supposed that that was the normal and right thing for her to say and I scarcely gave it a thought as we drove over the ruts back to town. If she was at all nervous or worried, she never told me. And it's only now that I wonder.

Aunt Liza was probably the last of that generation of slaves, a woman who'd lived an incredibly long time. She was, if not venerated, at least greatly respected, and certainly known by everyone in town. She died in the spring of 1942, on a rainy Sunday and my grandmother and grandfather went in best clothes up to the AME Zion Methodist-Episcopal Church where she had gone every week since, I guess, Emancipation Day. It wasn't considered proper for little boys to go to funerals back then, unless it was your mother or grandmother, maybe, but I was told that the church was crowded. I'm sure it was. She must have been a fixture and a reminder of a past that I do not pretend to remember, neither in our kitchen nor throughout Princess Anne.

I see now a set of social responsibilities in it all. They were not outspoken, not something talked openly about like your obligation to put flowers on the graves of the Confederate veterans on Decoration Day, but something as absolutely real and binding as your belief in the goodness of the Golden Rule. If you were white and lived in Princess Anne and had any money at all, then you were expected to give work to the colored people in Princess Anne. And when they were too old or too sick to work for you any longer, you cared for them and looked after them. Patronizing, perhaps, and certain to make some people angry today. But back then, neither I nor anybody else drew these sorts of moral judgements. It's just the way things were done.

Like the Ten Commandments, these responsibilities were perpetual and everlasting, through good times and bad times. Dimes and quarters weren't easy to come by in the Depression, at least not in the house where I lived and where Aunt Liza and Lucretia worked. Back in the twenties, I guess, people had money and the price of produce held steady. But the Depression hit hard about the year I was born. We weren't without money but every dollar was earmarked for a worthy cause before it was ever earned. And one of the top-ranked worthy causes, right next to county taxes, was the few dollars to pay Lucretia and Aunt Liza. It was probably no more than three or four dollars a week at best, but people would have cut back on food to make sure that those dollars were there on Saturday for their help. The help had no other source of money.

* * *

I grew up knowing black and white people equally well. In a town of only a shade more than 1000 people within its corporate limits, it's hard not to do otherwise. I shared my sandbox with Toussant James, a little four-year old who belonged to Pauline who worked next door. We built great things together and he tormented me and I tormented him and we both laughed about it. He stole my ice cream one hot summer day and I locked him in the privy in retaliation. We both got spanked by our respective parents.

Along with Lucretia and Aunt Liza, there was Lit Davis. Lit was a perpetual presence in my life. His real name was Littleton, an atavistic reminder of some sort of previous condition of servitude to the well-to-do Littleton family of a century before, but this had been shorted to Lit. He was half AmericanIndian, half Negro, a big, strong, protective sort of man whose skin always shone red in the sunlight. When I was nine years old, Lit taught me to shoot a twenty-two caliber rifle and how to bait a fish-hook so that I could fish for inedible sunfish at the town bridge. Later, when I got my driver's license, Lit taught me to wash a car just as well as he did at Henderson's Gulf Station, a skill I still hold better than most people. Lit was always around the house, doing the heavy work that my grandfather was too feeble to do without protest. He took down the wood stoves in April and put them up again in the fall. He changed the living room from summer straw rugs to winter carpeting and beat them out and put them in storage in the barn. He helped my grandfather with the hog slaughter and sausage-making every fall. When he'd get drunk on a Saturday night, it was my grandmother who'd get him out of jail on her recognizance and make sure that he showed up before the justice of the peace later in the week.

Lucretia Holbrook was second mother to me. Just as young and trim and just as imaginative as Mother, she was an endless source of exciting stories, of ideas, of great things to do. If something went wrong, I'd come crying to the closest of the two. She was unable to read and write when she came to work for us at twelve years old in the late `twenties, but my grandmother and my Aunt Ethel took that defect into hand quickly and taught her. She picked it up with amazing speed. Soon she read everything at hand and retained an amazing amount in memory. She kept the habit through life and, with innate goodness, manners, and natural grace and dignity, she became one of the more well respected, educated and literate women in Princess Anne. My grandmother spent her last night on earth in Lucretia's company, talking and reminiscing and planning a bridge party in Ocean City for the next day. Lucretia was with my mother through her last years, not as servant but as friend. Even today, as a spry, quick and agile woman of more than eighty-five, she remains a great and dear friend, the only one of those big people from my childhood still left alive.

Lucretia became a caterer in later years, and I stop to think ... Lucretia, indeed a strange name, full of irony for one who's life has been spent in the preparation of food for others! But on the Eastern Shore when she was born and needed naming, nobody took Renaissance Italian history very seriously, and the name of Lucretia, associated as it was with *Lucretia Borgia* (whose unpleasant specialty was the poisoning of elegant food for her enemies among the nobility of Europe) was lost on all of us. Because she loved to iron, because she has specialized in those hard-to-do formal dresses with hundreds of pleats, department stores in Baltimore and Philadelphia still send her unfinished garments for their final pressing and trimming before delivery to customers. She swears she has never slept more than four hours a night at any time during her life. She gets up at three in the morning and reads until it's time for breakfast, a truly remarkable woman. It would be hard for anyone to feel superior to her. Much more likely is a feeling of awe.

* * *

Even in the best of times, so far as I can determine, Somerset County never had a real "monied" class, no aristocracy whose only claim was their fortunes. You knew people who worked small truck farms, or watermen who fished and crabbed in the summer and worked oysters in the winter. You knew well-off merchants and bankers, politicians, and carpenters and teachers. There was a natural aristocracy of sorts, but its base rested more on accomplishments than on wealth. There was no entrenched wealth, no country clubs, and no Cadillac or Packard agencies within miles.   In this, we may have been different from other areas of the old tidewater South.   And just as this must have made a difference in the tax revenues, it also made for a difference in the way those of one race treated those of another.

Today we would say that this was a mutually dependent society based on a symbiotic relationship. I wonder what my grandfather, George W. Brown, would have said if he could have heard such a thing. Back then, thank Heaven, such words had no particular meaning and were not in fashion. We didn't say anything, black or white. It was just that they were your neighbors, like it or not. And you couldn't afford to offend somebody today whose help you just might desperately need tomorrow.

For reasons lost, if not to history, at least to me, many black people in the County were property owners. That meant considerably less than the name implies. It generally meant twenty or thirty acres of fair-to-moderate truck-farm land, a dilapidated gable-roof two-story clapboard house of four rooms and a rickety wooden unscreened front porch. It would sit like a blemish on the landscape with the plowed front field running all the way up to the door. Behind would be a barn in equal condition, along with the privy and a well. A driveway to the County road was less of a driveway or a lane than a place where crops couldn't grow because that's where they always drove the wagon team.

But it was their farm. And just down the road a half-mile or so would be another farm just like it. And it would be owned by a white family. Its roof leaked as badly in a fall rain and the termites ate at the under-pinnings of both with equal enthusiasm. Both farmers worried about dry weather in July, bean prices in August and school shoes for the children in September, and both hoped that the well water would hold. It was hard to feel superior.

The ferrier in that part of the county was an old black man. He was the only one who would come out to your property and shoe a horse so that you didn't have to walk the poor lame creature into town to the blacksmith shop on Beechwood street. You treated him with respect if not great friendship because he was an elder in the Colored AME

Church, carried weight in his community, and it wouldn't do to get half of the county down on you. And he treated you with respect (if not great reciprocal friendship) too, for if you were white, he needed your business. It would do no good to get the other half of the county down on him. Not with a family to feed.

We knew each other, those of both races. We knew our virtues and our shortcomings. We knew who could be trusted and who was inclined to put on airs, something that very few of either race took much store of. We had grown up with each other, most of us. I remember a story in the local *Marylander and Herald* during 1944; one of our white sons, serving in Italy, homesick as he could be, recognized a familiar black face in the cab of a truck somewhere north of Naples. It was one of the black sons of Princess Anne. "I never thought I'd ever hug another boy," he was quoted, "`specially not a colored boy."

All of these "symbiotic" relationships shouldn't ever be misread and lumped under the heading of equality. It wasn't and anyone who does, would do so at his own risk. The motto wasn't equality. It wasn't even separate but equal. It was separate and dependent. The two races interacted in many ways, and the results were generally favorable and beneficial to both races. They also stayed separate and the results seemed also to be beneficial. The strictures, the guidelines, the social niceties and conventions seemingly had existed forever and so far as I could tell, would go on forever.

I learned them early on as a child. Aunt Liza was elderly and respected. I'd call her Aunt Liza as I'd been taught. It would have been as foreign for me to call her "Missus Dennis" as it would for me to call her Liza or for her to call my grandmother "Tillie" rather than Miss Tillie. Lucretia, being younger was, is, and will always be Lucretia to me. Naming had its meets and bounds and ceremonial determinations. A maid would refer to a white lady as ... say, "Missus Smith" but after working in her kitchen for years, she would call her "Miss Ella." It was a liberty taken and granted with accepted ease. And it was hallowed and sanctioned by time. The title was always appended.

Churches were segregated and everyone was happy. Everybody knew his place of worship. There was no inclination to have interdenominational church services. White Baptists wouldn't go to the white Saint Andrews Episcopal Church under pain of conscience, and they certainly wouldn't go to the colored AME-Zion Methodist-Episcopal Church over on Broad Street by the River. Why should they? That was the colored church. It would have made everybody feel uncomfortable and out of place. Exceptions were weddings and funerals. And there it was limited to closest of friends. But yet, everyone respected all of those houses of worship. You kept your voice down and didn't laugh and shout as you passed in the street, particularly if there was a meeting or service going on inside. It was not only good manners. It was just the way to act. You could walk through any graveyard, but you would never step on a grave, regardless of the previous color of the occupant.

Schools were segregated. The idea that they should be otherwise wouldn't have made any sense. Why should they change? There was Princess Anne Elementary School off of Beckford Avenue and Greenwood Elementary School on the southern outskirts of town. It was an accepted fact that they'd get our old books, a real shortcoming in the system because we didn't have enough money for new ones ourselves. But we had to part with them after three or four years, ready or not. Each school had dedicated and loving teachers who maintained iron discipline.

The social strictures penetrated into all kinds of corners and crevices of life. It was a hard thing to codify. The best you could do was to pick up a sort of sixth-sense about how to act and what to say. The rules were as subtle and as pervasive as the Samurai Code of conduct.

Calling on the house of someone of the other race had a protocol which we never forgot. Politeness required black people to go to the back door of a white house and knock. You'd then enter through the kitchen, state your business and most likely stop, talk and laugh a little over the affairs of the day.

If you were white, you simply went into the front yard, stood a few feet from the porch and called out the name of the person you wanted to talk to. They'd come and you'd stand outside in the heat or cold and state your business, unless the two of you were on very close terms. Then you might be asked to come into the front room.

Christmas was a special occasion. Lit Davis would show up around eleven in the morning. My father would always have something ... generally a few cigars wrapped around with two or three dollar bills. Lit would feign surprise and Dad would often break out a bottle of Bourbon and offer him a Christmas drink. This was accepted gratefully with no undue surprise on his part. Lit's counter-offer would be heart-felt: "Mr. Frank, can't I gather up some of this trash here for you and take it back to the shed? And maybe bring you in an armload of wood?"

Lucretia was hired as a matter of course and showed up on Christmas afternoon to help with dinner. She brightened the kitchen considerably with her wonderful, happy and perceptive nature. She was paid, of course. I don't know but I always felt that her gift was in the nature of some extra and very special dessert.

There was much interaction, but there was one overriding stricture, a line that was never crossed, to the best of my knowledge. A person of one race never interfered with the social life of the other. It would have made everyone uncomfortable. It was live and let live. Miss Frances Hickman would go to the house of the colored family down the road on her farm and care for a bedroom-full of sick and feverish children, but there were no mixed parties, no integrated dances, no family parties shared on either side of the fence. The only black people at a white dance could be the musicians who seemingly had special dispensation to take a few more social liberties with white folk, keeping their banter in the style of Duke Ellington. But having been raised in the music business and having played at dozens of dances, I can't recall a situation when an all-white band would have played at a solely black social function. Perhaps they had a patent on all of the good musicians and just didn't need us. I don't know.

You didn't compete in athletics. Intermural sports were, almost by definition, between two white schools or two black schools. But that seemed to hold only for competitive sports. Hunting and fishing were something else apart. Although not common, a white man might go deer-hunting or down on the marsh to bag a few geese with his colored neighbor. Both of them could use the extra food on the table. And a man with good bird dogs or retrievers was always in demand, regardless of his race.

If you were an oysterman, a captain of a skipjack, you'd hire on any man strong enough and dedicated enough to handle the dredge or the oyster tongs, regardless of his color. On the deck of an oyster boat it was equal employment opportunity at its best. And strength and endurance was the great equalizer among men.

If you were a young black man just graduated from Greenwood High School, you might become a barber, but you were the "colored barber" and you'd not be hired to work your trade in a white barber shop with a white clientele. However, the sister of the same young man might become a beautician whose customers were exclusively the gentrified white ladies in Princess Anne. This defied logic but was perfectly understood by the conventions of the time. Nor, if you were a merchant, a men's clothier, as an example, would you hire a young black man to serve your white clientele. But you'd hire him to work as a waiter in your restaurant and be glad to get him. Still, you'd not take him on as a bartender in your beer hall, the assumption being, apparently, that eating was necessary but drinking was purely social. I do not know; I only speculate.

Black people and white people didn't, if they could help it, ride on the same seat of a car together. Rainy nights when my grandmother would drive Lucretia back to her house, Lucretia would climb into the back seat behind the driver and they'd chat and gab all of the way home. Right-hand front was permissible only if you had a two-seater. The same stricture held if a black man drove. The white people rode in the back seat.

I lived in that town for twenty years while I grew to adulthood. During that time, we knew of one absolute barrier that affected everyone: interracial dating. It didn't happen and everyone would have been shocked if it did. I knew of every possible confession that any boy in my social world might reveal. And not once did I ever hear of an interracial anything involving boys and girls in Princess Anne. It may have happened, and people were simply too self-conscious to talk about it. But self-consciousness was not a highly prized virtue back then. Honesty was. Readers may convince themselves that I am either naive or was blinded to the reality of it. Be that as it may. These readers may be factually right. I only know what I was and wasn't told.

There was, as most people know, a strong social structure in both communities. The two structures existed independently of each other. And each could be cutting within its own framework. A sense of right, wrong, and good conduct was pervasive. The phrase that white people used to describe the other parallel community in town, if they were properly brought up, was invariably "colored people." The term "darkie" was only rarely heard, in spite of literature to the contrary. To call a man or woman "black" would, in that day, have been a grievous insult to the other. "Nigger" was never used by any white person with breeding and good manners, at least in addressing them. It would speak poorly of yourself if you slipped and used it in their hearing. That particular term was one used by colored people to describe one of their own who was beneath their contempt.

At the top of the social structure on one hand were the white people who owned the stores and the bigger farms around Princess Anne. They generally lived in those substantial white frame homes on South Main Street. Princess Anne College, the "colored college" a few miles east of town provided aristocracy aplenty for the colored community and the only Ph.D.'s in the whole county, so far as I can remember. They were respected greatly and were, on the whole, lovely people. The president of the college, Dr. Kyhe, was always referred to by that title by everyone.

There were a few independent colored businessmen in town. Jim Dennis ran a bicycle sales and repair shop which, when gasoline was short during the War, prospered greatly. His wife Gwendoline, a gentle and soft spoken lady, had the only beauty parlor in town and as such was the confidant of all of the white women. And there were artisans, carpenters and painters and bricklayers, none of whom were rich but all of whom seemed to fare as well as their white counterparts.

Even through the softening lens of years, I'd never hold it to be a model of how American society should be fashioned today. The inequities were vast. It was just that people accepted them more philosophically, leaning heavily on the biblical beliefs that, if justice isn't done here, it'll be carried out in Heaven. Job opportunities were limited and whole professions were out of reach for the brighter boys and girls in the colored high school. And I couldn't be everywhere. I didn't see everything, the injustices, the tears, the intentional and unintentional insults. I didn't see the last lynching in the State of Maryland which took place in 1933, right up on South Main Street. Although I've asked countless times, I still don't know anything about it at all, because everybody, black and white, was too ashamed to talk about it.

The town wasn't perfect. Our race relations, although we never used that word, were far from perfect. But after forty years of serious integration efforts, of methodically tearing away the old structure, it's still not perfect. If I were to return from the dead in years hence, it would probably not be any better.

It was better than a lot of places. Better perhaps than the Northern cities, the class-ridden counties of South Carolina, better than Mississippi, maybe even better than Tidewater Virginia. To be perfect would have required that all of us, the black and the white in that little town, be among the angels.

And nobody in his right mind ever made that claim about Princess Anne.

Guns, Gunpowder, and My Right to Enjoy Them

Besieged as we are, if I can use an inappropriate metaphor, by the anti-firearms forces in America today, it's hard to recall a time and place where guns, hunting, and target shooting was neither opposed by the gun-control people nor supported by the NRA. On the Eastern Shore of Maryland, such things as guns simply existed. They weren't discussed nor argued.

I grew up around quantities of firearms of all sorts, rifles, a few revolvers, but mostly shotguns. I never gave them much more thought than I gave to axes and hot wood stoves and gallon cans of kerosene. They were simply things that the adults had and used and about which children such as I were dutifully respectful. They could hurt you but probably wouldn't if you didn't fool with them.

Nearly every house I knew, ours, and those of most others I visited, had a shotgun, either propped up in the corner of the living room or more than likely, standing by the kitchen door. Just as obvious were the boxes of Remington or Springfield shotgun shells, little cardboard boxes emblazoned with colorful lithographs of braces of quail and slaughtered ducks. The shotguns were utilitarian, bottom-of-the-line things, bought at Taylor's hardware store. They were much more functional than beautiful, with plain maple stocks and blued barrels devoid of ornamentation or other expensive, self-conscious fanciness. Cared for well, even a standard-model shotgun would last a man for a lifetime, and I can recall antiquated models with side-mounted hammers that men who were old had bought in their youth. No reason to buy something newer when that one did just as good. The traditional double barrel, twelve-gauge model was the favorite because it was cheap and devastating. My uncle owned a twelve-gauge Browning automatic shotgun with hunting scenes engraved on the breech, but he was from Washington and not from the Eastern Shore.

Shotguns and rifles weren't, as some contemporary writers would have us believe, the physical manifestations of some strange psychological need to assert masculinity on the part of my elders. Nor was that shotgun in the corner a futile attempt to revive the rough-and-tumble values of the Old West, something about which most of these elders knew precious little and cared about even less. Guns were quite simply the normal tools and implements of their trade with which farmers and watermen worked every day. Not to be skilled in their use was like not really knowing how to harness a team to a wagon, or how to really plow a straight row of corn.

A part of using these tools properly came from an almost inbred respect for their inherent lethality. Whatever it was, it seemed to work well because in growing up, I never heard of more than one or two gun-related accidents. Guns just didn't "go off" and kill people. Wild charges of buckshot didn't just blast across a crowded kitchen and kill all of the innocent within hearing range. Just as you grew up with a deep respect for the back ends of the pair of mules out in the barn, you grew up with a respect for firearms. It was taught to you and bred into you from the time you could walk. Accidental shootings, we believed, were the sole property of the visitors who came from the city every fall to hunt deer in the swamps and forests outside of Princess Anne.

* * *

I, like all little boys in Princess Anne and everywhere else in the United States at that time, grew up with a steady feeding of cowboy movies. Saturdays were traditional and if Mr. Earl Morris ever showed a Hopalong Cassidy or Tom Mix movie, it was on Saturday when the kids were free to pay a dime to get in. Revolvers were a part of it and Fox's five-and-ten sold dozens of cap pistols of varying quality every month. As a six and seven-year old, I bought my share. But even then, the older boys would count the rounds that Bill Boyd fired from that blazing Colt pistol of his and laugh loudly and knowingly and derisively as he discharged the seventh and eighth blast from his six-shooter at the bad guys. The older boys among us knew revolvers almost as well as they knew shotguns..

But paper-cap guns, as we all knew, were toys. So, obviously, did my grandfather, a man who was a rough-hewn grandparent and wonder-fully indulgent with me. He apparently cared very little for the refinements and niceties of civilization which were foreign to anyone down there who was born in those marshes before the Civil War. One of the few recollections of strong and stern words from him came because of my misuse of a paper-cap gun. I'm not clear on what happened, exactly but in a great, screaming, fast-draw gunfight with Ralph Dryden or somebody, he brought it all up short with a shout to me: "Hey! Don't you ever point that thing at nothin' you don't want to kill."

I explained the obvious to him but it was useless. The word "toy" had no more impact on him than if I'd spoken it in Greek. "I don't care. You never point a gun at nothing living unless you want to kill it." It broke up my day, and that I can remember very well. I was not used to having my grandfather holler at me. He never had before and never did afterwards.

A few days later, after thinking about it some more, he told me that he'd buy me my own "real" gun for my ninth birthday, less than a year away. And he did. And the surprising thing, as I look back on it, that his decision was not questioned by anyone, either in my family or anyone else in town. Nine years was an age where a boy had better learn to shoot if he was ever going to. But for a lost battle before you ever begin, try this as a subject for a letter-to-the-editor or a human-interest article in your local suburban newspaper today.

I rifle-shopped the Sears and Roebuck catalog almost all of that previous spring. My fancy was a Mossberg twenty-two caliber automatic, a mean, sophisticated-looking weapon that held a huge tubular magazine of bullets, a rifle which could fire as fast as you pulled the trigger. It was thirty-two dollars, I remember. I told my father that this was my selection. Here, he interjected himself and common-sense reasoning into this whole gun-purchasing issue and forbade it. No nine-year old was going to be given a semi-automatic weapon and that was it! The scope of my target shooting was reduced to a single-shot Remington target rifle, a lovely, well-made and well-balanced rifle which retailed at Sears for only $19.95.

I was furious for a few days. My dream of spraying .22 caliber lead all over the marsh behind the house as fast as I could pull the trigger was shattered. That I was as sad and destitute as I was probably justified my father's attitude completely, at least in his mind. Any kid who wants an automatic just to see how fast he can shoot it probably had just proven that he shouldn't have an automatic weapon in the first place. He, of course, was absolutely right.

But it was a memorable day when I got it. There lies the utility of a gift like that to me: the visions it brought to my mind on that first day of ownership, of hours and hours of target shooting, of hunting, of developing skills and determination and a steady hand. And there are the intangible benefits too: the absolutely unforgettable smell of a new gun fresh from its packing, the solid clunk and thud as you placed it stock-down in the corner and the fact that it was so much heavier, with so much more heft to it than I'd expected, having been at close terms only with BB rifles. I loved the quiet, no-nonsense click of the bolt as I'd chamber a cartridge, the smooth precision look of the chamber, blued steel polished to a micron or so of absolute flatness. No cheap pot-metal casting here. From that time onward, cap guns were the property of the youngsters. I was, by gosh, nine years old. And all of this before I'd ever fired the first round from it.

I'd bought a Hoppes rifle-cleaning kit as well, a thing with its own lovely smell and before I'd ever fired the first round, I had my cleaning kit out, polishing the blued steel barrel to an even more brilliant and lustrous blue. And I oiled the stock to make the polished walnut shine more deeply. It was beautiful, the most beautiful thing I'd ever owned. And it was mine.

My grandfather and Lit Davis, general handyman around the property, took on the job of teaching me to shoot without killing myself or any of them. But thinking back on it, I think that I took that rifle very seriously. Those previous little lessons and familiarity with toy guns played with properly had done their job well. I handled it with instinctive respect and safety. One or the other of those two men would hand me a .22 caliber "short" cartridge but only after I was pointing the rifle away from me, from them, from the house, from anything except the far bank of the marsh.

Like many other things in those days and times, there was the formal and proper way of doing things, and the way we did things in Princess

Anne. There were no paper targets properly erected on target frames at the far end of a carefully measured target range. To do so would have been completely out of place. I remember that one or the other of them put a one-pound coffee can on the ground about a dozen feet in front of my feet and told me to shoot it. I cannot remember the details of that first shot. But I can remember various unhappy shouts from me when I missed: "Nothing came out!" And the memory of other coffee cans, shot at various distances until they were more hole than can stays with me. I liked coffee cans much better than bottles, another favorite target of young boys. Coffee cans would bounce and spin when you hit them. Bottles shattered and that was it. Just broken glass.

Having a river directly behind the house was an asset that other boys didn't have. It had a natural embankment to form a backstop for bullets. And an empty coffee can tossed over the bank at flood tide made a wonderful moving target. Any can with a screw-on metal top was an enemy ship needing to be sunk. "Hit it twice," Lit told me. One to let out the air and t'other to let in the water."

Shooting was fun for the whole family, and I remember Sunday afternoons after dinner when we'd all gather out back by the river and shoot. Neighbors brought over an odd assortment of rifles and in a good day, we'd dispose of two or three boxes of twenty-two caliber bullets. Bottles, cans, old cartons, anything handy would serve as a target and six or seven adults and one small boy would take turns shredding, shattering, or sinking whatever seemed most convenient. Looking back, I suspect that a part of the turn-out had less to do with target shooting as much as to watch me, a combination of childish, shrieking enthusiasm and brow-wrinkling icy determination.

Sundays were the days. The Sabbath was generally kept holy down there and stores were closed and beer wasn't sold. Baseball wasn't played in general. But quietude never seemed to extend to target shooting, at least in our family. Nobody considered the intermittent little "pup-pup" reports to be a desecration of the Sabbath. But Saturday was the day to stock up on ammunition. A box of fifty .22-caliber shorts cost twenty cents. Longs were twenty-three cents and a box of handsome, formidable looking long-rifle bullets cost a whole quarter. They seemed worth the difference in psychological terms if not in hits on the target.

Ammunition was available at Mr. Tom Taylor's hardware store on Broad Street, just a few minutes' walk from home and hardly a Saturday passed that I didn't venture into that remarkable old establishment. Long before I was born it had been a livery stable and when cars replaced horses, Mr. Taylor, with minimal work and expenditure, had converted it to a hardware store. It was quite unlike any hardware store you are likely to find anywhere today this side of the Yukon. It had a wonderful smell about it that those of a later generation will never know. Hemp line, rope, plow blades, boat anchors, nails, plumbing pipes, boat oars, paint, caulking, kerosene, and ammunition and guns were everywhere. Their location was sort of casual, roughly wherever Mr. Taylor could find an uncluttered spot. Only he could have operated that place. Nobody else would have had a life-expectancy long enough to allow him to learn the stock.

He was a kindly old man, always dressed in a black suit, stout, balding, and stooped and he took a liking to me. I had questions about guns and ammunition that he seemed happy to answer and he'd always show me everything he had in stock, even though I only wanted a box of .22's. He had ammunition which must have been a generation old, things that maybe a customer had asked about and never bought. He had eight and ten-gauge shells for huge old punt shotguns, veritable cannon which were mounted on the gunwale of a skiff and used to hunt ducks on the marshes until such artillery was outlawed in 1919. And boxes of deer-rifle cartridges of a size that nobody bought anymore. He even had a little box of steely-looking percussion caps for muzzle-loading shotguns, which he showed me. "They's still folks down toward Deal Island uses `em, even today."

Shells and cartridges were, in those Depression days, sold "by the piece" because most of Mr. Taylor's customers didn't have enough ready cash to buy a whole box. He took to giving me some of these antique shells and cartridges as a present, to go with my box of .22's. I collected a whole cigar box of them, .330's and 30-30 cartridges, and .22 Hornets, and .44-caliber revolver bullets and a fearsome looking cylinder of brass and lead called a ".45-90" which, the old man assured me, "was for killing elephants, or at least, buffalo." I'd spend rainy days looking at each one, enjoying its heft and weight, memorizing the numbers stamped into the brass, and dreaming about owning a real gun which would shoot something as impressive as they. To a large extent, Mr. Taylor, as old and feeble as he was, gave me a cataloger's interest in firearms which, even today, is still with me.

* * *

Somewhere along in those days just before the War began, my uncle from Washington, a great hunter and fisherman, discovered among his vast collection of guns a small .410 shotgun. "It's not a 410-*gauge* shotgun," he told me. "Just say .410 and you'll be right." It seemed to be surplus so he gave it to me on indefinite loan along with boxes of shotgun shells. The 410 is a boy-sized shotgun, about two-thirds the weight and about a quarter as effective as those double-barreled 12-gauge shotguns that adults used for any serious shooting. But I was delighted. The 410 got me away from the river bank and its fixed targets and out into the fields.

We had hunting licenses in Somerset County, but being practical people, the people in the County offices who issued such things didn't include little boys with small shotguns. This left me free to roam the back fields behind my grandfather's farm out on Somerset Heights. Before anyone cut me loose to hunt on my own, I was told what was perhaps an obligatory story about Phil Smith's only son. I'm sure everyone in Princess Anne was told approximately the same story, a story which was sad and terribly true. Phil Smith, a gentle old man who had served haltingly as the town undertaker for a long lifetime, had lost his only child, his son, in a hunting accident back in 1916. The boy had made a fatal mistake of climbing a fence or leaving a rowboat (it seemed to vary with the teller) and had kept his shotgun loaded with the breech closed. Somehow, the trigger or the hammer got caught in something and his gun went off and killed him on the spot. The moral of that story was clear to me: Always walk with the gun broken open, never closed unless you sighted birds, and then and only then would you cock the hammer. And <u>never</u> hand your gun to anybody unless you break it open first. "And," added my grandfather, "Don't you never take one, neither, 'less it's broke open." My grandfather taught those facts like they were nothing except good manners. Decent people just don't do it any other way.

That in a nutshell was hunter safety. I'd already learned never to lay any gun, my rifle or this shotgun, down so it touched the ground muzzle-downward. (*"Sure to get mud in it and stop up the barrel and it'll explode and kill you."*) Thinking back, if everybody followed those three simple rules, there'd be fewer gun accidents in the field worth talking about.

There I was, a ten-year old, walking the back fields of my grandfather's farm, bright sunlight, dry clean air, and hundreds of birds and eight or nine shotgun shells in the pocket of my corduroy jacket. Birds had no political lobby of any consequence back then. Those smaller birds native to the Eastern Shore were limited to species so few that you could count them on the fingers of one hand. We had great quantities of sparrows and almost as many blackbirds and starlings. Robins, catbirds, mockingbirds, jays, and cardinals were in considerably shorter supply.

My grandfather, no Audubon, conveniently grouped all of these birds into two categories: those that ate his seeds and those that didn't eat them in vast, arrogant quantities. The first category he hated because they were destructive nuisances. The second, he placed in the categories of good birds, especially the "mockers" because he liked to hear them sing at night. He didn't like crows. Nobody did, for they could un-do a morning's worth of planting in ten minutes flat, but he was wise enough not to include them in the list of George-Brown-protected species. Crows could take care of themselves without his stewardship. He knew as well as anybody that nobody could get within firearm range of these wise creatures, and so they weren't worth his time to categorize.

Blackbirds, the red-wing and all-black types, the starlings, and the sparrows were each worth a nickel bounty if I'd bring them home. This more than covered the cost of the .410 shells, even the high velocity type, but only if I were a good shot. The object, so far as I was concerned, was to maximize my return, with no concern about "unfair" shots. My tactic was to catch them sitting on a telephone wire or fence post, as still as possible, and disciple myself not to fire at all if they took wing. I had been told by those who were older than I that sitting birds were unfair game. A great hunter shot them on the wing but deep inside I knew that I was not a great hunter. I was happy if I could be just an effective hunter. Of course, it wasn't that I hadn't tried to shoot birds on the wing. The reason I was a miserable failure was that I was shooting with a tiny little gun with a full choke barrel and a thimble-full of shot pellets, just about the poorest design that one can use for wing-shooting. But nobody told me.

It was a different world, and guns and ammunition were a sane and sensible part of it. When I was in the sixth grade in 1943, I hunted dogs. Yes, dogs, to the present-day anguish of all Friends of Animals and gun-control people everywhere. Clarence Laird and I went hunting wild dogs at his farm down at Venton. It was a bright Saturday morning in late winter and packs of dogs had been creating havoc with Mr. Laird's livestock. Something had to go, either the dogs or his chickens.

We went out equipped with a pair of .22 rifles and Clarence took the old Chevrolet flat-bed work truck and drove us to the middle of a large field. We climbed up on the back, a safe distance from the ground, rifles in hand, sat down and waited for the dogs to appear. As I recall, we didn't have to wait long. They were big, angry, snarling hounds, combative to their core, a dozen or so of them, all of indiscriminate breed, more than a match for any calf and a toss-up challenge to anything that walked on two or four legs. In a short time, most were dead and the survivors had run off. Clarence and I administered the *coup de grace* to the injured and left them for the buzzards. Then Clarence, all of 12, climbed back up into the cab, cranked the engine over and we made our way back to the house.

Indeed it was a different world, back then in the 1940's. One can only smile with hidden delight at the noise, commotion, and indignant editorial outrage that we would have caused, had we shifted our actions forward a half-century or so. Two elementary-school aged boys, driving off in a truck by themselves, both armed with rifles and belts of ammunition, and using their best judgement in the *ad hoc* execution of a group of criminal dogs. There's enough there for everyone to hate, for great righteous indignation, home visits from social workers, filing of criminal and civil charges, and perhaps even an injunction or two from the local courts directed against our parents. We would have made the evening news.

But then, Mr. Laird was just happy to get rid of those dogs. And he seemed to be convinced that these two boys had done a good job.

Wetlands - from the Inside Looking Out

A glance at any topographical map of Somerset County will prove one fact to the observer: That there is no shortage of wetlands. Stretching from a point at the Inlet at Deal Island to another point almost half way to Princess Anne, we see vast areas marked as marsh. Crisfield is surrounded by marsh. A vast network of marshes and swamp surrounds the Pocomoke River to the south. If the Eastern Shoreman takes the current laws and concerns over wetlands preservation a bit casually, he is to be forgiven. Though law-abiding, he can scarcely change the padlock on the chicken coop behind his house without infringing upon one aspect of the law or another. Riverlets and guts cross his fields. Creeks wend their way through the thread of pine woods at the back of his property. Mud-holes appear from nowhere by the barn every spring and predictably dry up again in July. There's nothing rare about a wetland, so far as he can tell. The Eastern Shoreman has been fighting a losing battle with wetlands and marshlands and swamp since his first forebears arrived on these shores three centuries ago.

Back in the early 1940's when Sunday Driving was still a universal family social event, I remember a drive with my grandfather. Sundays were the only times he'd willingly submit himself to the confines of an automobile, much preferring his horse and carriage for everyday transportation. We set out due west from Princess Anne, on the State Road to Deal Island. The farmland immediately to the west of town was as good and productive as any in the county, light, sandy soil just made for truck crops. Drive past that and you come to the pine timberland which is almost a hallmark of many areas of the lower Eastern Shore, light second- and third growth white and yellow pine, interspersed with small farming communities ... Oriole, Venton, Champ, Saint Stevens, and Monie.

But beyond that is marsh, almost all the way down to Deal Island. It was this that caught my grandfather's eye. To those who grew up elsewhere, an Eastern Shore marsh doesn't offer much justification for enthusiastic sightseeing. The marshes are vast, friendless expanses of low broad-leafed grasses, reeds, cat-tail and marsh-mallow cut through by little drainage guts[1], unbroken by the slightest hummock or hill, mostly flooded on high tide and covered by mud-flats on low. In summer's heat, they reek of rotted, salt-laden vegetation and in winter they are pure, beautiful desolation.

An Eastern Shore Marsh - Hot and uncomfortable in summer, cold desolation in winter - and by nobody's most charitable definition, a hospitable place at any time of year.

"Over thar'" my grandfather said, pointing off to the south. "See that old piece of a frame house standing by that pine tree?" I looked out of the left-hand window. A third of a mile away across that marsh, the bare, weather-beaten bones of a two-story clapboard house were silhouetted against a gray, winter sky. "That there's the old Tyler place. When I was a boy," he continued, "that was one of the best

---

[1] A *gut* is a local word for a small, naturally formed drainage channel, usually defined as one narrow enough to step over. The term is universally used on the Eastern Shore and the Chesapeake regions, and apparently not used elsewhere to any great extent.

farms around here. Old man raised `berries, corn. A real good farm."
He paused. "But then the marsh come in," he added in explanation.

At ten or so, it seemed impossible to me that anybody could have
raised anything in that wasteland. I envisioned it somehow just as it
looked to me, but with the house all back in good order and rows of
beans and strawberries planted among the marsh grasses and muskrat
holes. That was before I knew about the "sinking `Shore", a place of
continuing geological change, equal but opposite to its social and
cultural permanency. Continued pumping of fresh water from the
underground Susquehanna aquifer has caused the top-lands to sink
down on themselves, just as a boat lowers and sinks by the pier as the
tide beneath it goes out. High-and-dry lands become wetlands, farms
give way to marsh, and marshes fill in with sediment from up-Bay and
new islands and flatlands are born. Geologists chart and measure,
hydrologist engineers drill and drain, and environmental protection
lawyers file creative injunctions for whatever side they favor, but to the
old-line Shoreman like my grandfather, it was just a part of nature's
cycle, as God, the Old Master had planned it. *"The salt marsh come in
and takes it and then the marsh dries up again."* It requires a long-range
view to assess it like that, but that's how it was seen.

* * *

I came to know the marsh first-hand, in ways that many Eastern
Shoremen never know a marsh. They live next to it, they sail boats
around it and through it, they drive past it, and hunt geese at its edge,
but most of them don't know the marsh or fire twenty-two caliber rifles
into it for target practice as I once did. But I know it. I worked in a
marsh for an entire summer.

It's best to use the word "in" rather than "on" because it's considerably
more apt and descriptive. And so it was, that in June of 1948, with
high school behind me and college staring me in the face, I needed a
job, one which was better-paying than those which all young boys were
expected to take from the time they were ten or eleven "to teach you
the value of hard work and money, and that nothing comes free."

College grants and tuition scholarships were almost unheard of in the 1940's and, for most of us, if we wanted to go to college, we were expected to earn our own way. As I saw it, four-to five hundred dollars wasn't an excessive amount to lay aside for my freshman year, and besides, I had to consider the cost of my first car, a used Hudson-Terraplane with an unforgiving thirst for oil. Truck driving, which I had done illegally and without a shred of State sanction at fifteen, wasn't steady enough work, playing saxophone in the local dance band was a Friday and Saturday night occupation, and the local soda fountain at Daugherty and Hayman's Drug Store was disgracefully poor paying.

Mr. Ballard Miles had the answer. Mr. Miles was the official Somerset County Surveyor, a position which, I recall, placed him unopposed on the local ballot at every election and guaranteed that he'd have no competition for county and state work. I had a long history of work with Ballard Miles, for when I was seven and playing down by the town water-pumping station, he'd given me a dime to hold a long rod called a "stadia" while he peered at me through a telescope-like thing. What he was doing made no sense to me, but it wasn't hard work for the few minutes involved. And it was the first dime I ever earned from anybody outside of the family and I still remember it. I was delighted.

I'd always liked Ballard Miles since that first day. A small, wiry man with black eyes and dark curly hair, a high-energy, clipped way of speaking, and given to almost safari-like styles of dressing, Ballard Miles was probably one of the best, most honorable, and brightest men in the entire town as I later came to appreciate. I honestly don't know if I asked him for a job or if he asked me if I needed a job, but I can remember it well, his explaining to me that we would be surveying Busby's marsh. And I'd carry the stadia rod for him, at ten dollars a day.

Ten dollars a day needs perspective: For an eight-hour day, it works out to a dollar and twenty-five cents an hour. In that distant day, the minimum wage, where it was enforced, was twenty-five cents an hour. I had driven a panel delivery truck running soft drinks and cheap candy to Ocean City the previous summer for fifty cents an hour and was the envy of everybody. I was ready to go through fire for ten dollars a day. I was almost ready to go through Busby's Marsh.

Busby's Marsh, he explained to me, was down past Monie at Dame's Quarter, almost to Deal Island, and the State Government wanted it surveyed so that they could turn it into a game preserve for waterfowl. I looked at a map of Somerset County a few days ago, and there it is, a massive, irregularly-shaped parcel of land, marked with those little grass-like swamp symbols that cartographers use, and labeled *State Game Preserve*. The name Busby has disappeared from all records apparently, but in my heart, it will always be Busby's Marsh. I know those jagged, angular property boundaries and I looked at them on the map. I put them there, I thought to myself. And a flood of memories came all at once.

"It's not easy work," Ballard had told me. "If it were, I'd not be charging so much to do this job and I'd not be paying so well. And here's what we'll be doing." He then gave me a course in the rudiments of surveying, paying attention to the job of stadia carrier, my job. And then he told me other things I needed to know.

"Do you have waders?" he asked me. I'd never heard of them. High-top gum boots were my specialty for splowing around in the Manokin River. "Never mind. I've got some extra ones that'll fit you. And a canteen?"

I had nothing except one from my Boy Scout days. "Get one, a big one. No. Better get two. You'll carry all of your water for one day in those. And don't bother to pack any lunch." This was strange, I thought, but then I remembered a small country store, `way back on the State Road. Maybe we'll eat there, I thought.

Days began early. Ballard believed that you could do better with an early start so that you could be free of the marsh by the heat of the afternoon. The first day, I recall that he wanted a really early start. On the drive down to Busby's Marsh, he told me not to worry. "I want to get our today's readings finished before the tide comes in. It'll peak around four this afternoon. We don't want to be wading around out there in much more than three feet of water." It was then I realized the real reason for the waders. This wasn't to be a marsh-bank expedition. It was marsh, all the way.

We left the car, and what amounted to civilization, back somewhere on a meandering oyster-shell road. Ballard's practiced eye spotted the correct parking place on this desolate road, based in all likelihood on a line of sight with a distant landmark. We unpacked the trunk and shouldered the equipment we'd need. I had custody of the stadia rod, a long, telescoping wooden pole with a roll of metallic tape with numbers built into its front face. I had no clear idea how the thing worked or how it fitted into the science of surveying. I knew I'd learn as much or more about it than I'd probably care to. But for the moment, I remember that my mind was more fixed on the morning sun. It was to be, as we often termed such clear, airless, but humid summer days, "a real scorcher." Busby's Marsh, and everything its damnable name would ever imply to me, was fast becoming reality.

Far to the southwest, miles it seemed to me, was a lone pine tree, perhaps a survivor of the antediluvian days of a century before, perhaps the most hearty surviving seed of a pine cone dropped in disgust by a passing sea gull. I don't know and didn't stop to consider the philosophical implications at the time. All I knew was that the tree was our destination. "We'll take the first readings over there," Ballard told me.

The marsh was work of a nature I'd not forget. We set out on a course directly for that tree, stepping into knee-deep water as we left the oyster-shell roadway. The bottom was soft mud. I had my two canteens slung safely over my shoulders, up as far as possible from the water. The reason for the "no lunch" requirement became wonderfully clear to me at that time. Stadia-handling was a two-handed proposition. There was no place to carry lunch above the water line. And there was no need to plot anything but a straight course to that tree for there was only marsh between us and it. It varied not at all on any point of the compass.

A rod-carrier's job involves lots of walking, about twice as much, by my imperfect calculations as that of the surveyor himself, for the surveyor sets up his transit instrument and his note book on a conveniently suitable site. The rod carrier then walks to a point perhaps a hundred or so yards to his rear. The surveyor makes a reading from the elevation and location of the rod-carrier's stadia and when he's satisfied, the rod carrier picks up his instrument, circles past the surveyor and walks to a point perhaps a hundred or so yards to his forward side where another set of readings are taken by the surveyor. Ballard Miles' job was to record compass bearings, estimate distance and calculate his elevation based on the position of my stadia rod. My only job was to carry the rod and hold it stark still while he made his readings. This process is repeated time and time again, perhaps a hundred times or more, according to my own imperfect recollections on that first day down there on Busby's Marsh. I could have been wrong. But it seems like it.

It wasn't a simple walk, those hundred-odd yards. Within my first hour on the marsh that morning, I'd stepped into some sort of a subterranean hole and shipped water into my waders. "Don't concern yourself overly much," Ballard called out. "The water won't hurt you. The waders are really to keep off the snakes."

I've often wondered about people who have an abnormal fear of snakes. I didn't then and I don't today. I have a healthy respect for snakes, will avoid social contact with them at reasonable cost, and I'll never set out to antagonize them in the least. Live and let live was my guiding principle. I'm glad I held to those principles for we had a marsh full of them, black snakes, water-moccasins and cotton-mouths, mostly, and a few other unidentified species which qualified as general-purpose snakes in my mind.

In general, live-and-let-live applied to the snakes as much as to me. Two or three steps forward and up ahead a few yards you'd hear their characteristic "spluch" as they'd sliver off a mud hummock or from the branches of a foot-high marsh sapling, seeking shelter in the water, no more anxious to meet me than I was to meet them. There seemed to be a great deal of mutual respect exercised between those snakes and me.

It grew hotter as the morning wore on. Mornings in those open swamps will run you ninety or so degrees. Afternoons will be a bit warmer. By ten thirty, my first canteen had been opened and drained.

It was a practice which I repeated each day out there on that marsh, swearing each day that in the future I'd ration myself and not do it again tomorrow. But I had a weakness for water and I always lacked the moral fiber to resist drinking it if I had it. I realized early on that there was a benefit in not having food out there on the marsh. Food would have made me thirstier. I wracked my conscience thinking of George Washington, who also began his life as a surveyor, and wondering if the history of our Nation might not have been different if he'd begun his career on Busby's Marsh and not working for Lord Fairfax on the clear, elevated, and inspiring heights of the upper Shenandoah Valley.

But there were beautiful and thoughtful sights right out there, heat and mud and stench notwithstanding. Flocks of red-wing blackbirds suddenly would swirl up from some hidden thicket of marsh reeds. Sounds were magnified, or so it seemed. When you are standing motionless and steady for long minutes while the surveyor takes yet another reading for good measure, the sound of a frog dominates your sense of hearing, for that's all there is to listen to, and you hear him with an interest and an attention to detail that you'd never give to him back in civilization. And you can marvel at the Divine ability of those little water-walking insects which can scurry across a smooth surface of marsh water with no more effort than we can walk across the road, and I'd envy them that ability and wish to Heaven that surface tension would keep my own feet out of that damnable mud bottom. I found that even the fish swimming in the shallows make their own peculiar sounds. And herons were never native to Princess Anne, but here on the marsh, you could see ten or twenty each hour, standing and looking stately and noble and disdainful at the world. Muskrats were every-where and if you ever yearned to see where and how they live, Busby's marsh was the place to do it.

There's a myth held by people who've not been there that mosquitoes and insects are worse in the morning and evening hours, but it's not true, at least not on Busby's Marsh. There, from Monie Creek to Dame's Quarter, they reign supreme at any hour of the day or night. They liked us. They were all probably starved for a good meal and Ballard Miles and I were the only two warm-blooded mammals for miles around. The word got around and they took advantage of us.

Toward mid-day we'd take a break from work. Not a lunch break, but a break anyway. Ballard would try to lay us at a rare high spot in the marsh if possible, but this often took some planning for most of the "elevations" were below sea level and, according to local standards, a genuine "hill" might have a certifiable height of six or seven inches above. We'd talk and he'd show me the rudiments of surveying, how the trigonometry of his measurements needed to work out and how, after surveying all day and coming back to the spot you started from, all of your measurements had to square with themselves so that when you made up your map at home during the evening, your same starting and ending points of the circuit were at the same place on your map. "Wouldn't do otherwise," he told me, stating the obvious.

If mornings were bad, dismal, and filled with minor torments, afternoons stood unparalleled in their ability to inflict human suffering. The sun would blaze in a clear, overheated sky, raising both temperature and humidity to near intolerable levels. The sour smell of the marsh was everywhere, although by afternoon, we'd both become so saturated with mud, salt, and decaying vegetation that we'd become adjusted to it. But if any one discomfort stands supreme in my mind, it was thirst.

Before that time, I'd often been thirsty. Now I was not only thirsty, but I carried thirst to a new level. I knew thirst for the terrible, mind-engaging, character-dominating thing that it is. Towards two o'clock on any afternoon out there on the marsh, every thought I had was framed somehow with a deep association with water. I'd seen it in the movies, the lost cowboy, seeing the mirage on the desert. It's true. I can recall one blistering afternoon, soaked with brackish water and empty of canteen, when I saw one of the most beautiful scenes that one could see on that marsh.

The sky was a bright July blue, ornamented by a few classically shaped cumulus clouds and we'd just rounded a bend to see a singular grass-covered islet in Fishing Creek, surmounted by a lone hardwood tree, perhaps the only one for miles around. The grass was an incredible green, unlike the flat marsh-colors our eyes were accustomed to. And the tree was perfect, young, well formed and glistening with health. Like a tree in a meadow, I thought. And as I did, the words of a then-popular song came clear and filling into my mind: *There's a tree in the meadow, with a stream drifting by ...."*

I knew that there must be a stream, somewhere up there, a fresh-water stream of clear and cool fresh water in the shade of that tree. Reason told me that water, if any, would be as saline as that in which I was standing. But the thought of that tree and its stream-drifting-by dominated me and I couldn't get it out of my mind. Right then, at that moment, I'd have given up my day's salary if there were indeed a stream, and I could rush right up to it and drink it dry.

By three on almost any afternoon, Ballard Miles would be willing to call it a day and we'd slog back the mile or more to the oyster-shell road and his waiting Chevrolet sedan. I'd pull off my waders and replace them with the dry shoes and socks I'd abandoned early in the morning. The thirst I'd try to thrust to the back of my mind. It wouldn't be long now.

The junction of the main road to Deal Island and our oyster-shell feeder road was a mile or so away across the marsh. And right there at that corner was one of those typically run-down, disorderly country stores which, at the time, substituted for a convenience store ... one small room, odd shelves full of canned stuff, shotgun shells, white bread, cigarettes and chewing tobacco and not much more. I cared not a thing for anything inside. But on the rickety front porch was a soft-drink dispenser of a sort we no longer see. Cooled only by ice, it wasn't much more than an ice chest with a mechanical gate. One nickel allowed one swing of the gate and you could slide your choice out and free.

I remember that rusty soft-drink chest, full of moldy water with a clarity and near-reverence unequaled by any other mechanical object. For nearly three months, it became my Holy Grail, my object of veneration during those hot, scorching afternoon hours on Busby's Marsh. And every afternoon between three and four, I made my pilgrimage. Like a person possessed, I'd leap from the car, run up to the porch, fumble a nickel into the slot, and withdraw a *Nehi*.

For those unfamiliar with the term, a *Nehi* was pronounced "knee-high" and was the product of the Nehi Beverage Company. Nehi was the producer and proud vendor of the biggest, most generous soft drink of that period. Whereas Coke was content with a six-ounce bottle, and Pepsi-Cola boasted twelve ounces for a nickel, Nehi outdid them all in quantity if not in quality with sixteen ounces. In rural parts of Somerset County where people set great store by quantity, Nehi outsold everybody. Nehi produced fruit-flavored soft drinks of varying garish colors, minimal carbonation, and maximum sugar. Nehi wasn't necessarily my drink of choice, but it was available at that little country store. In quantity.

Like any other good Pilgrim, I'd developed a ritual procedure. Slamming a nickel into the slot with a maniacal fanaticism, I'd grab the first Orange Nehi bottle in queue, rip the top off and drink the entire 16 ounces - straight down without so much as a pause for air. I've drunk great beers in Europe since then, but nothing, even today, could equal the sheer orange-coated pleasure that the first Nehi of the day would afford.

That was for starters. Another nickel, another orange Nehi, this one to be savored and drunk at leisure in a sitting position on the old wooden porch. Ballard would have his own Nehi and we'd break out a pack of dry cigarettes and matches and each would sit while the mud dried. And then we'd drive back inland to Princess Anne. I'd go in the house, smelling none too good. No fond greetings this time, not at all. Just a simple "throw those clothes in the bucket and go take a bath."

* * *

Marshes are everywhere down in Somerset County. We called them marshes, not wetlands, but it makes no difference to the Eastern Shoremen or to the great sky-filling flocks of Canadian geese who feed and breed there, or to the hunters who still make a ceremonial trip once or twice each winter to their duck blinds, or to the trappers who trap muskrats and export their pelts to Russia. The marshes have their own particular charm on a cold raw winter day, with the perfectly dried reeds, marsh ferns, and cat-tails rattling in the wind, a few desultory mallards trying to gain a wing-hold in the gusting air, and scuddy low-flying clouds hanging out over the Bay, presaging a certain change in the weather. Weather like that can make you wish immensely for home and a warm kitchen and fried oysters and muskrat stew. And you know that it all wouldn't seem half as good to contemplate if it weren't for those cold, wind-chilled marshes out there.

And there's a colorful beauty to them in the summer too ... if you're not waist-deep in them as I was when I worked to lay out the property lines on Busby's Marsh, and you have cold beer in the cooler and you're a spectator in a fishing boat lying a hundred yards off shore. The fish depend on these wetlands for breeding and the birds need them for nesting. Walk them waste deep as I did and you know that they're not the dead and sterile places you see from the roadways. They're crammed full of life forms, from the microscopic to the size of snapping turtles. And, on at least one occasion, a surveying crew.

That summer on Busby's Marsh defined it for me and gave me an appreciation of wetlands in a way that all of the people in Baltimore who belong to the *Save-the-Bay Foundation* will never truly understand. At the end of a day, while we'd sit and smoke a dry cigarette, drink our Orange Nehi, and glory in the drying warmth of the afternoon sun, Ballard Miles would pull out his oil-skin notebook and show me a sketch of the meets and bounds of the marsh we'd just worked. "Right here," he'd say, "is the old Bozman property. Tomorrow we'll look for that brass bench mark they say is set down there on the fence row ... just about here, and then we'll strike a south-east bearing line from it to intersect the head of Broad Creek. That'll mark Mr. Bozman's right-hand boundary line. And from that line straight out to the west, it's all marsh."

Of that, I had no doubt.

A Bridge of Time and Place

The building of the Chesapeake Bay Bridge was, at one and the same time, both a great joiner and a great divider. Most people who lived on the Eastern Shore of Maryland as I did in July of 1952 saw it as a joiner. Geographically, we had now, for very practical reasons, bridged ourselves over to the rest of the State of Maryland. But future generations of sociologists and people who study such things may view the building of this bridge not so much as a joiner but as a divider.

If there was ever a defining watershed, a point in time where the new could be divided from the old, it was, so far as the Eastern Shoreman went, July of 1952. From that time onward, the insignificant little things which defined the Eastern Shore as a unique and rather curious entity

The Chesapeake Bay Bridge as it appeared on its opening day of July 30, 1952, a single, graceful span linking the Western and Eastern Shores of Maryland.

gave way. Culturally and economically, the Eastern Shore of Maryland is today not a great deal different from any other semi-rural area in the country from California to Maine. Nobody set out to improve and change the attitudes of the DelMarVa Peninsula. That's just the way it worked out. And it all started with the Bridge.

Before the Bridge, the defining cultural hallmark of the Eastern Shore of Maryland and its little towns like Princess Anne and Salisbury and Cambridge was its isolation from the rest of Maryland and the rest of the world, for that matter. It was a parochial place. And parochialism abounded, in customs, in the livelihoods and in the fundamental outlook of its people. The Bay was its western and southern frontier, the Ocean its east. Far, far away, a hundred or more miles to the north of Princess Anne lay its only land exit, a small neck of land at Wilmington, Delaware. Nobody drove that distance if they could help it. And certainly not over the two-lane highways which constituted most of the miles of what we then still descriptively called "stone roads".

If you really wanted off, you drove to the west and took the ferry across the Bay. The ferry was more logical because most people wanted to go to Baltimore anyway, Wilmington being considered something like a foreign country, a place you didn't go without an invitation. And a journey to Norfolk, the major city to the south, was a truly formidable undertaking. A hundred miles down the flat marshes of Virginia's Route US 13 and a major passenger and car ferry voyage across the roiling open waters of Hampton Roads was nothing to be taken lightly by anyone.

But once or twice a year, the Eastern Shoreman might have need to go to Baltimore. Business might take him because many of the wholesale seafood and produce markets were in Baltimore. Or it might be to shop at some of Baltimore's department stores, those which stocked more and better things than were available on the Eastern Shore. Getting to Baltimore from Princess Anne by water took the better part of a day and was a trip of such significance that it rated a few column-inches in next week's *Marylander and Herald*. The net result was that if you lived there, you rather much stayed there. Not only was the Eastern Shoreman a stay-at-home, he also had few visitors. It had been that way since the first white settlements sprang up there a good three-hundred years before.

The first of the settlers constituted the overflow, the malcontents and the scoundrels, as well as the ambitious of the Virginia Colony. My own first ancestor in America, a Scotsman from Glasgow named Alexander Brown, came up from Jamestown about that time. He'd served a long term as commander of the local militia and decided that life across Hampton Roads on the Eastern Shore might offer opportunities. So he became a self-styled "salt farmer" on the sandy shores of the Atlantic, collecting quantities of salt ocean water and distilling it for salt. This he sold back to the Virginians. Over on the Chesapeake Bay side, according to Captain John Smith, lay seafood the likes of which no European had ever seen, with crabs and fish and oysters there for the taking. And the alluvial soil of the Eastern Shore, built up mostly from hundreds of centuries of estuarine outwashings from the Susquehanna River to the north, was good farming property if you could get twenty or so miles inland, far enough to get away from the salt marshes.

Life wasn't prosperous for most people, but it was comfortable enough by the expectations of the eighteenth- or nineteenth centuries if you could stand the mosquitoes.[1] But comfort never seemed to be high on the list of people's priorities back then. It was enough to work hard and see it pay off in terms of a solid home, a property reasonably free of debt, and enough food on the table to feed the family. Most people worked the land or they worked the water. A few made their money as merchants and store keepers and carpenters or shipwrights. A few resorted to Bay-pirating and these were dispensed with when caught without too much concern and ceremony.

But there was nothing there to draw people in by the scores and hundreds. There was no gold, no minerals, no great natural seaports. Rail transportation was slow in coming. Good roads weren't high priority either. If you owned a boat, it provided you with a more comfortable and faster

---

[1] Because of the marshes, mosquitoes abound. Although Eastern Shoremen find them extremely annoying, many seem to possess an innate immunity to their bites and do not develop rashes or welts. It has been hypothesized quite logically that only those who held a natural immunity could have lived near these marshes. Those not so blessed found it impossible to remain. The survivors passed this immunity on to their children, an interesting example of natural selection taking place over a mere ten odd generations rather than millions of years..

trip to town than an ox cart drawn over muddy roads running uncertainly through pine thickets. The Eastern Shore was off the beaten pathway of the world. Nobody paid it much attention. And, the Eastern Shoremen were just as happy.

There was a time before television, about sixty or seventy years or so ago, when you could tell an Eastern Shoreman just by listening to him talk. They spoke differently, sounded differently, and what they said and how they said it was different from Baltimore, just across the Bay. It makes sense if you stop and consider it: His manner of speaking came from an amalgam of the speech spoken in Scotland and the British Midlands and Cornwall in the seventeenth century, and probably by the Jamestown colonists and other Tidewater Virginians. Its uniqueness eroded over the years, but for awhile, it was influenced by almost nobody else in the entire United States. If you never hear anybody else, it's hard to imitate them. Of course, the standard English of television has changed all of that now, for better or worse. Children now listen to MTV instead of Uncle Will, coming home and grousing after a "hawrrd day on that-`air ersh-ter boat".

I always believed, with some justification, that the Civil War brought about the first subtle changes. Some of the changes were in the way people spoke. My grandmother, who was born in 1884, as an example, spoke good standard, although slightly regional English. However, my grandfather spoke a heavy near-dialect, the one that everyone else in his family had spoken for two hundred years. But he was born in 1858 and learned to talk before the Civil War.

Before the Civil War there were few outsiders to bring in new ideas and new ways of thinking or of speaking. But then came 1861 when the Union troops arrived in quantity to occupy and protect Salisbury and the surrounding waterways against Confederate marauders. But I'm sure that the average Eastern Shoreman considered these fresh-faced Yankee boys not to be protectors, but occupiers sent to ensure that they and the rest of Maryland stayed Union. In this assumption, they were justified politically because the Eastern Shoreman, with his independent-minded agricultural background and suspicion of anything not home-grown, was a lot more comfortable with the loose control of the Confederacy than with the iron hand of the Unionists. Most of the people there would have welcomed General Lee or Joe Johnston with open arms and the Union forces knew it. The Eastern Shoreman was justified emotionally too. These foreign boys looked different, talked different, and probably questioned a lot of ingrained Eastern Shore assumptions. But in the end, the soldiers left their mark. The footprint is hard to distinguish. It could be that of an occupier or defender. But it's there.

My grandfather's only living recollection of the Civil War was nothing if not quaint and parochial. Living miles from Salisbury and the soldiers' encampment, he lived in seven-year old bliss and ignorance of it all, remembering only the day that the war ended and the soldiers marched down the road in front of his house, down to the Bay to be ferried to wherever it was that the Army would assign a demobilized soldier. "They come marching along and I was watching, standing there by the road barefooted to see the sight, and this little old green snake come up and I stuck my toe out at him and he bit me and I run in the house just a-holl'rin." George Brown was untouched by the Civil War, both in attitudes and in speech.

But the soldiers left and the Eastern Shore settled down pretty much as it was. Farmers farmed, watermen worked the Bay and the rivers. John Crisfield of Princess Anne did build a rail line connecting a little watering port in Somerset County, Somer's Cove, to the rest of the world, but not much else changed, except the residents of Somer's Cove were so overwhelmed and impressed by this technical feat that they gratefully renamed the town *Crisfield*. Later, Crisfield boasted of itself that it was the seafood capital of the world, a slight exaggeration, but not much, for the crabs, fish, and oysters from the surrounding bay brought prosperity to a few and jobs for many.

Along with good-quality truck crops grown in the light, sandy soil of the inland acres, the balance of trade came down slightly on the side of the Eastern-Shoreman, although not enough to create anything approaching a monied aristocracy. Solid middle-class was about all they could ever aspire to. And if one did become really well fixed, making any sort of a display about it would have been a little out of order. A man had to live with his neighbors from birth until they buried him, and it didn't do to set yourself apart from your fellow man too much.

By the time our generation came along in the 1930's, the culture, the life patterns were set. We elected congressmen and State senators and legislators, and bankers lent money sparingly and cautiously. Judges were sworn in and would always receive a tip of the hat from all of the hangers-on in the barber shop when they'd come in for a shave. People drove to town on Saturday nights to shop, first in horses and wagons and then in mud-caked automobiles. Little girls, the daughters of merchants, wearing organdy dresses, drove pony carts to no place in particular until they were big enough to have lawn parties and invite boys. The two newspapers, *The Somerset News* and the *Marylander and Herald* covered these events dutifully and people read them carefully to see that all the names were spelled right and nobody got left out.

The `Shoreman's local regional pride sometimes crossed a subtle line and became regional feistiness. Members of the Maryland House of Delegates rubbed it in when, over tumblers of Maryland Rye Whiskey in the local Annapolis taverns, they abraided the ears and sensibilities of their colleagues in the House and Senate by a raucous, repetitive chorus, sung to the tune of *The Old Gray Mare:*

> *O, we don't give a damn for the whole State of Maryland*
> *We're from the Eastern Shore!*
> *We're from the Eastern Shore, we're from the Eastern Shore*
> *Oh we don't give a damn for the whole State of Maryland*
> *We're from the Eastern Shore!*

And they didn't, either.

* * *

Back in the 1930's, the Shore was still mostly a land of working farms broken up by dense pine woods, with just a few little wood-frame country stores scattered here and there. They were ramshackled places with dark interiors and every exterior seemed to use the same metal lithographed bread signs for structural integrity. All of them could have used paint and most needed to replace the rusty screening in the front door. Where two or more such places stood within a hundred yards of each other, it was usually called a village. Add a Methodist Church and an Esso filling station and it was sure to be called a village and sometimes even a town, and the *Red Star* bus line might even schedule stops to pick up passengers. There were a dozen or so in Somerset County, places called Eden, and Marion Station, Fairmount, Costen Station, and Westover. And there were other villages on the Shore, villages with wonderful Indian names, left over from colonial times when there were still Indian tribes and the Indians hadn't all intermarried with the local stock. There were names like *Gingawkin, Matapeake, Kiptopeake, Tyaskin, Rockawalkin, Wetipkin, Chincoteague, Habnab,* and *Tonitank.* Most represented not a specific geographic location with marked boundaries but more often an area, or perhaps just a state of mind. People were generous with names back then and names cost little and meant a lot.

But if you drove down any of those long, straight single-lane roads leading through the cat-tails and marsh grasses and the brackish air, you'd come to the water. You couldn't help it. It was the nature of the Eastern Shore. If the farmers were independent-minded people, the watermen were twice their equal. They lived off the Bay. It was both home and work for them and their boats were everywhere. I can remember the fleets of skipjacks and bugeyes, work boats with either one or two masts, stretching as far as you could see across the harbor at Deal Island. Each was owned by a man whose livelihood depended on that work boat and so they were loved and were often given the names of women, a mother, or sister or wife and just as often preceded by the word *"Miss"*.

They used the feminine when they referred to their boats. They were invariably called "she". Traditional it might have been, but among the watermen, it was always so. It was so ingrained that they carried it over to other inanimate objects as well. Their cars and trucks were also feminine. And just as inevitably, a channel buoy was called "he". I offer no explanation.

"Raw-Boned" was the word we inland people gave to the watermen. By breeding and genetics they all were of a type, tall, lean, dark-haired, sun-baked men who were often bent and craggy and moved as though they were perpetually dodging under the swinging, arcing boom of their aftermast. Dredging or tonging the Bay for oysters in the winter is about the hardest and heaviest work a man can find, exceeded perhaps only by mining. Arthritis would hit them early and you could see why when you stood out on those docks in winter with a wet, cold wind blowing off Tangier Sound. The older ones often had dreadful skin cancers and it got a disproportionately high number of them. I can remember looking with seven-year old horror at old Mr. Keefer, half of his face gone, and as he explained to me unconcerned and not a bit self-conscious: "All us watermen seem to get it sooner or later. Don't know why. Ain't surprised none."

The watermen were determinedly independent people. To buy a boat, to recruit two or three other equally independently minded watermen to fish, to crab, or to oyster, took a certain strength of character. It took an abiding belief in yourself. And it also required a deep-seated belief in God, because God was, as many called him, "the old Master" who controlled the winds and the tides and the fearsome and sudden summer storms which, if they caught you, would sink your boat and kill you.

It was so even as late as when I was growing up on the Eastern Shore. These watermen at Deal Island and Crisfield believed with a fury and an intensity which would baffle many of today's theologians. It was a bargain that they struck with God: "I'll be to Church service every Sunday morning and Prayer Meeting every Wednesday night and I'll go to the Camp Meeting Revival every summer if You will just keep me safe out there on that Bay." In general, they kept their end of the bargain much better than God kept his. Accidents and drownings were frequent. Men were lost in the Bay and if they were lucky, someone might recover their bodies, or they might simply just be lost. People accepted it. Life, they felt, just wasn't always fair. They read the story of Job in the Old Testament and took it to heart.

* * *

From all I was ever taught or read on the subject, the Eastern Shore was a wild and dangerous place before the efforts of "The Parson of the Islands", one Joshua Thomas, brought Methodism to civilize and Christianize the place. A lot of the early immigrants to the area were social outcasts for one reason or another, having gotten to Virginia too late to get in on the original land grants and patents, or just plagued with bad luck. And for whatever reason, they came across the Bay to settle. Many seemed to have brought a bad disposition and violent temperaments with them, not surprising, because being on the outside looking in tends to make people evil-tempered.

Stories of pirates still abound ... not pirates of the high seas with the Jolly Roger at the masthead, but pirates nevertheless. They settled in the marsh land where fish were plentiful and they were never above mounting an expedition to way-lay a sailing ship beating its way up the Bay to Annapolis or Baltimore. And with a boatload of stores and barrels of whiskey and firearms, they'd make their way back home to the marshes and live exactly like you'd expect them to live ... until the stores ran out and the whiskey had all been drunk.

At the time of the Revolution, the local church was generally a continental branch of the Church of England, with candles and high services, an institution guaranteed to provide soothing spiritual aid to those farmers and planters lucky enough to have land and income but offering little in the way of uplifting spiritual guidance for such as those watermen. But Joshua Thomas changed all of that. In the early 1800's, with not much more than a log canoe which he named *The Methodist,* and what he considered a divine Charge from God, he brought them, or most of them, to Methodism. He changed the name of the place from what it rightly and aptly had been called for two centuries, *Devil's Island,* to the more respectible-sounding *Deal Island.* And just across the Inlet separating it from the mainland to the east, he changed the name of *Damned Quarter* to a softer *Dame's Quarter.* The Reverend Thomas wanted no such Godless names in his Charge. And his Methodist Church, with its uplift and good, singable music and its message, became a fixture from the first years of the 19th Century. It was the dominant institution in those days. Nothing moved, nothing changed, nobody lived or died, without the benefits of the Methodist Church. God was their lighthouse, as the old Methodist hymn went:

> *"Let the lower lights be burning*
> *send a beam across the waves*
> *Some poor fainting struggling seaman*
> *You may rescue, You may save..."*

And piracy became a thing of the past.

But it didn't decrease their fierce independence one bit. The watermen considered themselves a breed apart from every other resident of the shore. A man could work a farm. Or he could timber all summer in those steaming pine woods, battling black flies until he was ready to drop. But if you didn't work the water, if you didn't have their particular nasal accent, and if your skin wasn't like leather, well, you just weren't their equal. You were to be just a little bit distrusted. You probably thought you were somehow better. And that was something these watering people would never accept.

It held over well into my lifetime. Ask anyone of us from the "inland" towns like Princess Anne and Salisbury. Deal Island and Crisfield were not two places where we local boys would go to date a girl. In my entire growing-up, I never knew anyone from my class who dated a girl from Deal Island. I once dated a charming girl from Crisfield but only on a Sunday afternoon when the Church invoked a reasonably civilizing influence on the local boys. I could always tell the local Crisfield boys by the cars they drove, rakish things with the fenders rusted off, literally, flush with the body. (The salt air got to everything.) So, I took heed of my own safety and I was careful to sit on her front porch and not venture abroad. I never had a bit of trouble myself, although I kept a smart watch in my rear-view mirror on the long, dark, two-lane which led back to Princess Anne.

Princess Anne's high school played baseball against both Deal Island's and Crisfield's high school teams. If we lost, we were almost guaranteed right of safe and innocent passage out of the place, but winning was another matter. Fist fights were commonplace. Even in the 1940's, the watermen and their sons and grandsons were imbued with a pride honed just in the least by an unadmitted sense of "they-think-they're better`n-us. The Islander's centuries-old suspicion still lived.

But you could go to Deal Island in safety with your parents, all of whom must have learned long ago the drawbacks of mutual overt antagonism. And it was a picturesque, indeed lovely, place. It was an Island by virtue of that small channel no more than two dozen feet wide that cut it off from the mainland to the east. And once across the little wooden bridge, you could drive only a single road which led down the backbone of the place. Simple, frame two-story houses were, if nothing else, painted beautifully and lovingly maintained. It wasn't surprising when you considered that cleanliness and upkeep and annual painting was an ingrained habit of men whose lives depended on sound skipjacks and bugeyes for their safety and survival at sea.

You'd pass at least two of the Methodist Churches as I recall, one of which was founded by old Joshua Thomas himself and was distinguished by his own grave and those of generations of his followers. His was marked by an epitaph which we all committed to heart in elementary school. It was a rather indefinite but dolorous morality lesson in the futility of life and the inevitability of, one day, meeting your Maker:

Remember, Friend, as ye pass by
As ye are now, so once was I
For man is but born to die.

Those graves were not dignified by grassy mounds, as we knew proper graves to be in Princess Anne, but by the stark lids of cement burial vaults protruding a good foot above the ground. The land was too low to dig a proper grave and water would come in after a few feet. Stories have been told hundreds of times about the perils of being buried at Deal Island. A body just never stayed planted. One particularly scary one, which by all investigation is indeed desperately true, involved the huge storm of 1933 which flooded much of the island. A widow woman, who'd buried her husband only a few days before, was awakened at night by the sound of rising water around the underpinnings of her house. She went down the stairs to the first floor, lighted a lamp, and there she heard a quiet rapping at the front door. Thinking it was a beleaguered neighbor offering help, she opened the door to find her husband's wooden coffin in the doorway, floating free from the cemetery down the road. He'd come back home one more time.

At the end of the Island, past the small high school lay the little village of Wenona. When I knew it, it still had its own post office but I suspect that too has been consolidated with the rest of the County, as has almost everything else. Wenona was where the main harbor was, and it was a thrilling sight on a summer Sunday afternoon when all of the work boats were laid up for the day.

They'd lie at anchor there, dozens and dozens of them, the single-masted graceful skipjacks and the more formidable fore-and-aft rigged two-masted bugeyes. Many were older than the men who sailed them, having been built in the halcyon seafood-harvesting days of the turn of the Century and before. They were all work boats, no question, but they were all in good trim. Around the perimeter of the small harbor lay a handful of very

In later days, a solitary skipjack lay anchored at Deal Island, sails furled and rust staining her scuppers. The Waterman's traditional livelihood was in decline; the sturdy sailing fleets of a century before had disappeared, laid under by both nature and by changing times. (An original watercolor painting, *Deal Island Afternoon.* Artist - Becky Lowe, Crisfield Maryland, 1997)

utilitarian stores. I remember a grocery store where you could buy things for a packed lunch and fuel for the marine engines, and a sail loft run by a Mr. Brown. Somebody needed to be close at hand to make and repair sails. None of those buildings were anything but functional. The perpetual mud and the salt marsh air of Tangier Sound had taken their toll.

It was the magic of sail that has attracted people to that fleet of boats. Maryland fishing laws required that much of the oystering be done under sail and although they generally carried inboard marine engines, it was the sail that caught the eye and gave them an aura of romanticism that the old watermen themselves probably couldn't really understand. But that too passed away ... at about the time that Bridge was built.

The loss of the great sailing fleets of Somerset County can't be blamed on the Bridge entirely. You could stretch a point and perhaps you could make your case, although its end followed on the heels of the opening of the Bay Bridge by just a bit more than two years. People who lived through it will never forget it: Hurricane Hazel.

By the time she'd blown herself out in the upper reaches of New England, the Fleet lay in ruins. Work boats that had withstood the blows in 1933 and 1944 succumbed to the hundred-mile per hour gusts. The next day, when the sky cleared to a few scattered, scuddy gray clouds, almost all of the boats in the harbor lay wrecked and broken. Their stark wrecks lay there for years, rotting in the brackish water. Ten years later, you could still see them, corroded metal fittings still clinging to rotted wood. There was no sense in rebuilding, really. The Bay was in decline. An ecosystem which had thrived with perhaps a hundred-thousand people living on its banks and shores succumbed to the pressures of well over a million. Oysters in quantities which once provided ample income had been blighted by water-borne disease and their beds fouled by sediment and pollution. Crabs were only slightly better off. Besides, new jobs were on the way. Boys who might have "followed the water" as the expression went, looked elsewhere for jobs. And with the new traffic-flows from the Western Shore, they found them.

The watermen weren't the sole recipients of the Storm's energy. It hit everywhere and decimated the properties of waterman and inland farmer alike. Two-hundred year old hardwood trees were uprooted in wide swaths, not just an occasional one here and there, but great stretches of entire forests. Barns were leveled. It was almost as though nature, along with the wisdom of the Maryland State Roads Commission, had decided it was time for a change.

* * *

I was there the day they opened the Bridge. It was an accident and I'd certainly not planned it, for Eastern Shoreman that I was, I never planned such things. I was spending my last days down there on the Shore, the summer of 1952 after I had graduated from college. It was the last summer, the summer in which the Korean War had dictated that I was to go into the Service. The weeks had shrunk down into days. I took an evening off from my job in Ocean City as a night clerk in one of those barny old frame boardwalk hotels which, in an earlier day, had served the Eastern Shoreman's need for Eastern Shore vacation elegance in the long, sticky summers before air conditioning. Baltimore beckoned, and with my future wife at my side, we drove up the two-lane highway toward the Chesapeake Bay ferry slip. For reasons I can't remember, neither of us seemed to be aware that the ferry had ceased operations that very morning.

I remembered something about it as I drove up to where the ferry slip had been for as long as I could recall. There were police cars, and a few limousines with Maryland State Government license plates were stopped up ahead. With a few other cars in company, we drew up behind these imposing vehicles and came to a stop. It's the bridge! I remember reading that it was going to open this week, I thought. As we sat quietly, not being exactly sure what we were expected to do, a frowning Military Policeman gestured toward me with that standard, impatient back-handed move-ahead salute, and another state official walked up to my car. I rolled down the window and he presented my companion with an orchid corsage. We were, by count, the seventh vehicle to cross that span.

It was a beautiful sight, and I still think that the Chesapeake Bay Bridge is one of the most impressive achievements of the bridge-builder's art. No straight crossing course for it, for it curves gracefully and artfully in mid-span to head itself off to the northwest where its elevation soars high above the channel of the Bay. The suspensions are, in themselves, works of abstract art. I was impressed. There would be no more ferry with its hour-long crossing, no more lining up to have a deck-hand direct your car into the right lane, no more rumbling diesel sound to shake the deck plates, and no more hot dogs in the hurricane lounge. That I was truly leaving what had been my home for one last time was self-evident to me, even then. But I wasn't aware, when I'd return in later years, that "home" as I knew it, had also left on precisely the same day. It would no longer be there. If I'd been truly perceptive, I would have seen it not only as a watershed in my own life but one of vast greater importance to the life of the Eastern Shore.

There's a new day in view, and from that time on, nothing on the Eastern Shore of Maryland was ever quite the same again.

The Bay, once a formidable obstacle to transit, one which cost immeaurable amounts of time, was now no more than ten minutes drive, shore to shore. It put the farthest reaches of that Peninsula within easy driving distance of Baltimore and Washington. The Baltimorean could become as possessive about Ocean City as "his" vacation spot as any old-line shop-keeper from Salisbury. And business opportunities beckoned, an untapped market for builders and franchisers.

The political climate was changing too. Supreme Court voting-district decisions spelled the end of the political dominance of the Eastern Shore's Old Guard politicians in the State Legislature. Their songs rang hollow in the taverns of Annapolis, and nobody really cared any more that they were from the Eastern Shore. Cars, now enjoying the technical advancements of the fifties, poured across the Bridge by the hundreds of thousands in air-conditioned comfort. But more importantly, it was the trucks which brought the most profound changes. Goods sold in the local stores were homogenous and uniform with the rest of the world, the same brand names grasping at the same market share. The Eastern Shoreman was losing his unique identity. Television was creating the desire; the new shopping malls were there to fulfil it. The State was there to build the new highways to carry everything while the Shoremen cheered and applauded every new ribbon-cutting. The blacktops gave way to dual lane highways; new local spans were built to cross the network of small rivers that slice the land inward from the Bay. The Traffic Jam became the new hallmark, the new nemesis.

It remains there today, accessible to anyone over an impressive set of concrete overpasses and underpasses, dual highways and cloverleaves. It's a beautiful peninsula as you view it from the air on a clear day, hanging like a pendent from the mainland up around Wilmington and Philadelphia, the Bay and the Ocean to its flanks, its farthest tip suspended defiantly in raw open tidewater a score of miles from Norfolk, Virginia. But don't go out of your way especially to seek it out, trying to find the old oystermen with their skipjacks, or the solid, sweatsoaked and unpretentious farmers, or the garages where it was considered impolite not to stay and talk to the mechanic while he worked on your Chevrolet. And the same for all of those gentle people who fancied themselves and who actually were the pillars of the Eastern Shore way of life. It's no use. They've all gone away. That Eastern Shore is no more.

The DelMarVa Peninsula
and Maryland's
Eastern Shore

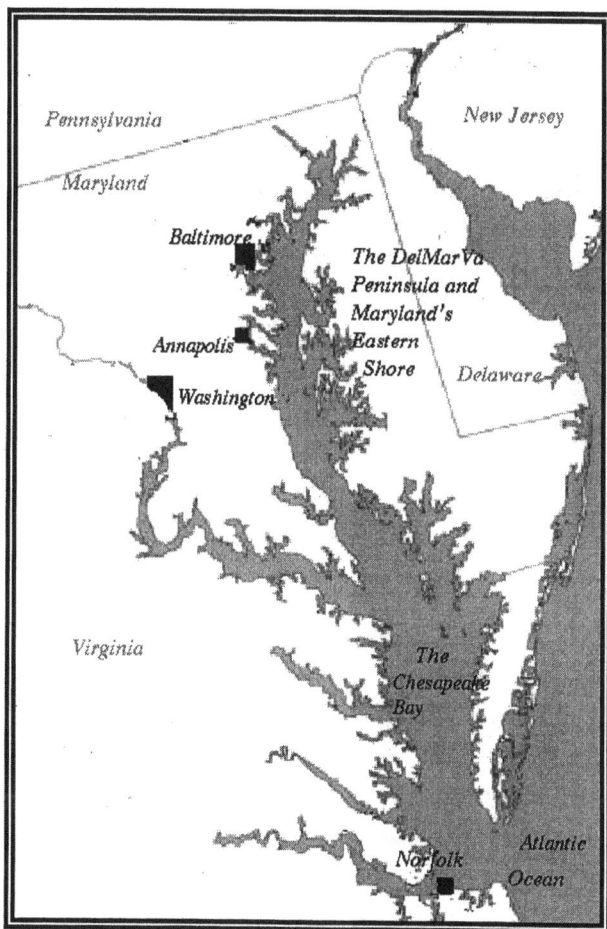

Somerset County lies just north of the Virginia State Line and fronts on the Chesapeake Bay. The three "fingers" protruding are the banks of the Pocomoke, the Annamessex, and the Manokin Rivers.

Somerset County
on the Eastern Shore
of Maryland

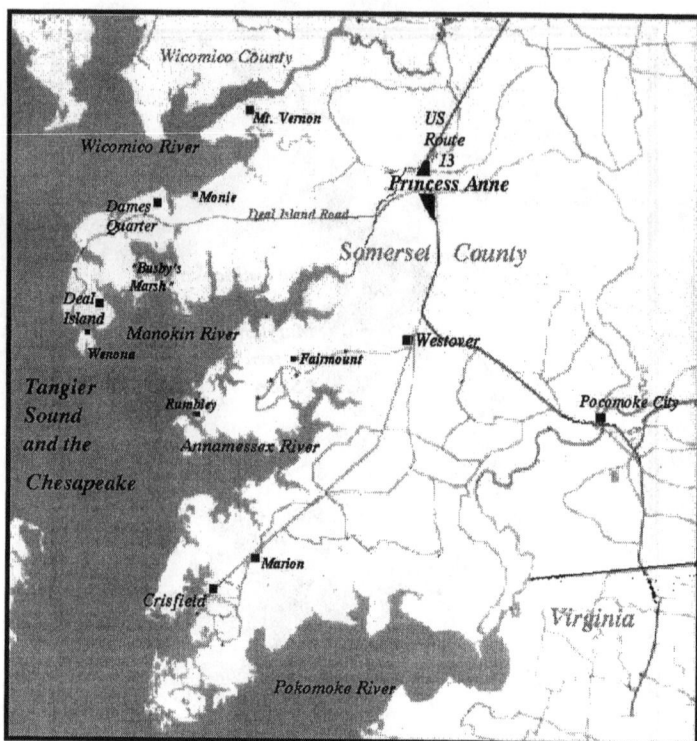

Picture Credits